Bearly Believable

My Part in the Paddington Bear Story

by

Shirley Clarkson

HARRIMAN HOUSE LTD

3A Penns Road
Petersfield
Hampshire
GU32 2EW
GREAT BRITAIN

Tel: +44 (0)1730 233870
Fax: +44 (0)1730 233880
Email: enquiries@harriman-house.com
Website: www.harriman-house.com

First published in Great Britain in 2008

The right of Shirley Clarkson to be identified as the author has been asserted
in accordance with the Copyright, Design and Patents Act 1988.

ISBN: 1-1905641-72-9
978-1-905641-72-7

British Library Cataloguing in Publication Data
A CIP catalogue record for this book can be obtained from the British Library.

We have done our utmost to contact all the necessary copyright holders prior to publication for all
photos and press clippings that are not owned by the author.

Printed and bound in Great Britain by the CPI Group, Antony Rowe, Chippenham.

For Ben, Emily, Finlo, Maddie and Katya

My raisons d'être

Contents

Foreword

I first met Shirley and Eddie Clarkson in 1972. I won't spoil Shirley's story by saying how that came about, but leave it to her to tell you in her own way, and in her own voice, for she has a distinctive way with words.

Bearly Believable is the saga of a Yorkshire woman's life, and her version of the events that followed our meeting as seen through her eyes. I say that because, like her late husband Eddie, Shirley embodies all the classic qualities attributed to people born in that part of the world: straight talking, afraid of no-one, a "what you see is what you get" approach to life. A spade is a spade, so what is the point of pretending it's anything else?

Being only human, they also – dare I say it? – have their share of faults. In Shirley's case there is a certain naivety too. First impressions are important, but accepting people at face value and taking them on without any references can have its drawbacks.

Bearly Believable is a very apt title for a book about the problems and vicissitudes encountered by the Clarksons, and Shirley in particular, while making what turned out to be an iconic three-dimensional version of a bear called Paddington.

Some of the people you will meet along the way struck me straight away as being the kind of hail-fellow-well-met character who might buttonhole you in a pub. Armed with a surefire tip for the 3.30 at Doncaster, and only too happy to relieve you of ten pounds; no, on second thoughts make that twenty…at a hundred to one it's too good a chance to miss…must rush and put it on before the start of the race…cheerio and toodleoo…say no more…my pleasure…

But then, I'm a Southerner, born and bred. We Southerners have nasty, suspicious minds. Also, it's easy to be wise after the event.

Underneath it all, Shirley's book, listing her many battles against bureaucracy and political correctness, says a great deal about how and why Great Britain, particularly the North of England, lost its position as one of the great manufacturing powerhouses of the world.

On another level it could serve as an object lesson to anyone contemplating starting up a business on how not to go about it.

And yet…and yet…

To this day, over the length and breadth of the British Isles and in many other parts of the world, Gabrielle Designs' classic creation lives on, bringing joy and comfort to individuals and families alike, looked up to, loved and respected by people from all walks of life, and that is no mean achievement.

It was summed up for me recently by a small item in the press. It seems that David Cameron was hosting a dinner party in a West End restaurant, and as they were about to sit down they realised there would be thirteen at the table. Shock! Horror! Who could they possibly invite at such short notice?

The problem was solved by the owner of the restaurant who went upstairs and fetched his Paddington bear. A fourteenth chair was produced and everyone was happy.

History doesn't relate who the extra guest sat next to, or what he had to eat, probably a marmalade sandwich, but somehow it says it all. Shirley has every right to rest comfortably on her laurels.

Michael Bond
February 2008

Bearly Believable

Introduction

I don't honestly think I've ever finished more than a handful of books, certainly not ones with small writing and no pictures. At the age of eight, I read 'The Secret of Spiggy Holes' by Enid Blyton, twice, followed by 'Ten Tales of Tim Rabbit'. After those I can't remember ever reaching the final page of any book.

Not being a book *reader*, it's slightly strange for me to be a book *writer*, but I was encouraged by family and friends to jot down my memories of Gabrielle Designs, and, before I knew it, the anecdotes had linked together to become a story.

Although 'Bearly Believable' is about *a* business, and contains some tips for budding business men and women, it is not a *business book*. If anything, it is a people book, amusing (I hope) and heart-warming, but not really educational. Given my record at school, the idea that I could write an educational book is stretching the bounds of credibility.

The people who appear in the book have made my life enormously rewarding, and I hope that I have managed to convey something of their character. A few were incredibly talented, charismatic, and successful, and those kinds of people are always fun to be around. Most were just ordinary people who never achieved anything remarkable – as measured by conventional standards – but who brought laughter into the lives of those around them. When all is said and done, that is a very big achievement indeed.

Chapter One – My War

I was born in 1934, and although it seems like only last Monday, I am amazed when my grandchildren come home from school and tell me they are doing World War II in *history*! They have days when they dress as refugees in Fair Isle tank tops, carry gas masks, and go down disused air raid shelters to eat spam and cheese sandwiches.

I was only five, but I remember 'The Day War Broke Out' in 1939. Mr May brought round a load of sandbags and a wheelbarrow of sand. My father, a GP in a suburb of Doncaster called Balby, showed no signs of the fear he must have been feeling. He calmly asked us to fill as many bags as we could, and then the war would end. We did, but it didn't.

That night, the siren on the roof of the local cinema sounded. I remember quite clearly the excitement of getting out of bed, crossing the garden and squeezing into the tiny potting shed which served as our shelter. It didn't have a roof, which was why it was considered safer than the house. Father would jump in the car and drive round to pick up Grandma and Grandpa from the next street. We all sat squashed around the wall on narrow benches. I complained about the smell of petrol, which was actually the brandy Grandma had drunk to steady her nerves for when the inevitable bombardment began.

Later on that year, we converted the cellar of the house into a sort of dormitory with two double bunks, and I was carried down there most nights. I don't know why they didn't make me walk. My father had chronic sciatica, and it must have been agony for him. We regularly heard the thud of the bombs falling on Sheffield twenty miles away, but we were never frightened. Even when a bomb landed in the street half a mile away, and Father was convinced the house above our heads had been flattened, he didn't show the slightest alarm. Apparently, when he climbed the steps, he was amazed to find that he could open the cellar door.

Aged five, I had just started school, and was a reluctant pupil. Most days, I had to be dragged there kicking and screaming. There were no such things as playgroups or nursery schools in the war, presumably because of a lack of teachers, so the first days of school, being torn from my mother's arms and thrust into this strange environment, came as a terrible shock to me. I remember the buxom Miss Hazleby holding air raid practice every day by leading us down to the cellar with a bicycle lamp strapped to her large posterior, saying, "All follow Mummy Bunny down the rabbit hole". This was the cue for us to put on our gas masks and make elephant noises. It seems obvious now that if we were able to blow air out through our gas masks, the gas could also get in, but at the time this didn't occur either to the children or, apparently, to the teachers.

One of my earliest recollections of kindergarten was the bullying. I was the bully. There was a very large boy – well fat actually – called Billy, and having taken a box of Maltesers to school one day, I found that there was one short to go round, so I made him do without. I was tiny for my age, but I dragged him into a quiet corner of the yard and brutally assaulted him. I'll go to my grave with that on my conscience.

It did puzzle me why there were large blocks of concrete piled at the sides of Balby Road. When I asked what they were for I was told that if Hitler landed in Hull (on the grounds, presumably, that it was the nearest port) they would drag the blocks across the road and stop him getting to Sheffield. Now, I was no war expert, but I couldn't see why Hitler wouldn't turn left down Alexander Road, go along Florence Avenue, and rejoin Balby Road further along.

My father, being forty, was too old for active service, but as a doctor was given a small petrol allowance. Most nights of the week after evening surgery he would go to the railway station to meet the troop trains that stopped in Doncaster, and as well as making tea and coffee for the soldiers coming home for forty-eight hours, he would drive them home to the outlying villages to save them time on their short leave. This kindness, on a foggy November night with no signposts and minimal headlights, was not for the faint-hearted. On the other hand, there were so few cars on the road at that time that the chances of him colliding with one were slim.

For my mother, on the other hand, the war constituted a kind of social merry-go-round. She was never at home. She spent every day selling war savings certificates, making camouflage netting, driving a mobile catering van around the searchlight stations in the area, knitting balaclavas and socks, or frying chips in the station canteen. After Girl Guides on Saturdays, I used to help her, taking the soldiers' caps in exchange for a knife and fork. My elder sister Pat and I were looked after by a wonderful character, a middle-aged man called 'Basset' who chain-smoked Woodbines, had a hacking cough, and sang 'Down at the Old Bull and Bush' continually. He may have had a Christian name but he was just Basset to us, and I never understood why none of my friends had a Basset too. How did they manage without one?

Basset picked us up from school, built rabbit hutches, washed cars, delivered medicines, cooked rice puddings, made all the blackout blinds for the windows, bathed us, put us to bed, and baby-sat for us if it was a night when Mother or Father were out on the street 'fire watching'. Can you imagine what the social services would have to say about that today?

'Fire watching' was an interesting concept. Based on the prediction that the Germans would soon be dropping incendiary bombs on Hall Flat Lane, a system of 'watchers' was organised. There were seven houses in our road, and the arrangement was that on the first night the husband from house number one sat in the car with the wife from number two; on the second night, the husband from number three sat with the wife from number four, and so on for the rest of the week. Perhaps I am being naïve, but it seemed a good idea!

When people ask me if I suffered in the six years of war, there are just two irritating things I remember. One was that a landmine blew the henhouse door open, which caused Pat and me to be late for school after rounding them up; the other was that I was fed up with having to keep quiet whilst the six o'clock news was on the radio. That just about completes my memory of World War II.

🐾 🐾 🐾

We lived next door to a family of three. The father had gone off to fight somewhere with the RAF, and the daughter, Pam, was my best friend. We played together every single day, mostly with my doll's house, knitting little vests for the occupants using darning needles and thin cotton thread. In the long, endless, hot summer days which we always had in the war, we played beside our ornamental garden pond, making boats out of peapods and walnut shells, in which we rescued water beetles in distress, or drowning flies. A long rope suspended from the ash tree provided a swing. I only wet my knickers twice as a child, once when I let Pam fall off the rope and she hit her head. I took her home and her mother walloped me. The other time was when my mother said I wasn't doing my piano practice properly, and she slapped me. Both instances live in my memory as terrible injustices!

On the days when Pam was my worst enemy, which best friends are wont to be occasionally, I spent my days playing 78s on the wind-up gramophone. 'Hush, hush, hush, here comes the bogeyman' and a Sousa march were my favourites, but I also loved Gilbert and Sullivan operas. I wore out hundreds of needles, and they must have been scarce, because they were all being melted down to make Spitfires. Big sister Pat in those days spent her life face down on the floor, *reading, reading* and *reading*. It made Mother angry – she thought Pat should have been knitting dolls' vests too. That's why, today, Pat is literate and well-read, and I'm not.

My limited artistic ability was somewhat curtailed during those days, because paper was in short supply. I'm not quite sure why – it certainly wasn't being used to make Spitfires – but Father always brought home the round, waxed lids used for the troops' coffee cups, and it was amazing what you could do with them with a bit of help from wax crayons or glitter wax, which was the old name for Play-Doh. Stick a safety pin on the back, and your jewellery box was complete!

My greatest delight was embroidery. Pat still has a tablecloth of lazy-daisy flowers which we worked on together. I remember that the red and purple flower in the corner was the subject of heated debate between us. Pat wouldn't do it how I wanted, so I bit her. Although she loyally didn't sneak on me, the teeth marks were a giveaway and Mother made me swallow a spoonful of Cascara (her remedy for bad temper) as a penance. I spat it out right down the front of my new smocked dress, and was promptly sent to bed.

I was playing ball with Pam when Mother came into the garden to tell us that the war was over. My only comment was "Does that mean we get a day off school tomorrow?" That evening we carried all our window blackouts to put on a large bonfire, with an effigy of Hitler on the top. Everyone was singing, dancing and kissing. I refused to kiss anybody because I didn't like that sort of thing, and it was a good twenty years before I overcame the aversion. Actually, I still have a loathing of New Year's Eve – all that snogging of strange men you've never met. I don't mind a peck on the cheek, but when they come at you full on, expecting a big mouth job – ugh!

My father revealed to us many years later that he foresaw what was going on in Germany in the thirties. He understood the way Hitler's mind worked, but no one would listen to him. Just imagine how history would have changed if they had! Long before 1939, he feared an invasion, and secretly buried four ampoules of poison in an airtight tin in the garden. He had no intention of his family suffering at the hands of the Nazis.

When my grandchildren ask me today which foods I don't like, they can't believe that the only thing I can't eat is marzipan. Dried egg, dried bananas, dried milk powder, even Brussels sprouts were a luxury when I was a child. I remember Mother swapping a hairgrip for an onion over the garden fence. Keeping hens, we had eggs of course, and grew a great wall full of loganberries, acres of peas, potatoes and tomatoes.

Sweets were in shorter supply. When I was away at school in 1947 we were only allowed six Smarties a week for our chocolate ration, and had to queue in alphabetical order, by surname, to get them. Being 'Ward', I only ever got black ones. My best friend at school, who I didn't like very much, was called 'Butler', so she always nabbed the orange and coffee coloured ones. You had to do someone's French homework for them to get their butter-pat. Thick pea soup and cold herrings after chapel on a Sunday night were a treat. We even feigned diabetic comas to get a spoonful of malt from Matron. I seemed to be the only person in the school that liked peanut butter, so my elevenses were well catered for.

Father must have worked incredibly hard in his early days as a GP. He started his practice in 1929 by nailing a brass plate to the door of our terraced house, and waited for patients to arrive. His first consultation, for which he charged seven shillings and sixpence, was with a pregnant lady. After it was over, he rushed off to buy a book in which to enter the details. The first hundred pounds he made, he lent to a friend and never saw him or the money again. But only a few years later, after the birth of his first daughter, Pat, he built himself a large four-bedroom house, with a bell fitted under the dining room table by which my mother could summon our maid, Florence. We came downstairs in the morning to find our breakfasts being delivered through the hatchway. This was either by Florence or the airman who she kept in the kitchen. It was a very comfortable upbringing. And of course we had a Basset.

Most nights I would hear Father opening the garage door and driving off to do a house call. The phone was by his bed, and he was on night duty seven days a week. Mind you, he never got up in the morning until after we had left for school. He just couldn't stand the endless screaming, "Where's my liberty bodice?"

In the latter part of the war, we gave lodgings to an army captain and his batman, and during his stay he contracted the deadly flu virus which was rampant at the time. He survived, but my mother caught it too, and was seriously ill. Although she recovered, it left her heart in a weakened state, which manifested itself in a terminal condition in later life.

It was about this time that my grandmother on my mother's side, a formidable lady, lent my father some money, presumably to help in the building of his new house, and then asked for interest on the loan. Mother was a proud and stubborn woman and told Grandma just what she could do with her money. Grandma was a Kilner, of the locally famous Kilner Jar family, just as stubborn as my mother, and this incident created a rift between them. It didn't help that I had been born a girl, when Grandma wanted a grandson, and the rift widened. They never spoke again, so consequently I never met 'Grandma Smethurst', or 'the Old Witch of Conisborough' as she was affectionately known in our family. I was too young to ask 'Why?' and was even quite proud of the fact that I had this mysterious grannie who lived four miles away that I had never seen.

Mother bottled jars of fruit in the war, like everyone had to before the invention of fridges and freezers, and I was vaguely aware that the jars used were called Kilner Jars, and were something to do with my grandmother. The design of the jar was such that when the glass lid was placed over a rubber seal, and the contents of the jar were heated then cooled, a vacuum was formed, and whatever was inside would stay fresh for years. This technique had been pioneered by my great, great, great, grandfather, John Kilner, and was so successful that by 1840 his company, The Providence Glass Works, was exporting bottles to America, Australia, South Africa, Ceylon, Bengal, and Madras from its factory in Thornhill, near Leeds. It had three warehouses in London and a fleet of ships. John's four sons, William, Caleb, George, and John, worked in the family business, but it was George's son, Caleb, born in 1845, who really carried Kilner to great heights. Bottles and glass containers of every description were churned out, and at the Great Exhibition of 1862 the Kilners took a stand and won a prize for a new design of wine bottle. (Presumably this is where my desire to 'exhibit' comes from!)

My parents' wedding day, 1930.

As a child, I did not know any of this history. We were comfortably off, but certainly not living like heirs to a giant industrial fortune. I later learned that the business collapsed almost as fast as it had grown. Failure to patent their designs, an expensive legal spat with local aristocrat Lord Scarborough, and competition from America dealt a lethal blow to Kilner Jars and the factory closed in 1937. An indication of the speed and severity of the decline was that when Caleb died in

1920 he left about 200 houses in and around Conisborough, and £11 million, in his will. Despite that legacy, his son George, had to take out a mortgage of £11,000 on his own house. The wealth simply evaporated.

George, I fear, was a waste of space. He had no business acumen whatsoever, and sat all day reading the 'Good Book'. He has obviously not passed his genes on to me. It was his daughter who was the estranged grandmother. My grandfather, on the other hand, did secretly come to visit us. He was a real miser, but full of fun. He once offered to *sell* my mother *half* a rabbit that he had shot. Probably poaching at the time.

At the age of ten I had just learnt to ride a fairy cycle! I was still a bit wobbly, being a slow learner at almost everything, and it was decided that our first post-war holiday should involve cycling to the 'Dukeries'. This may as well have been in Siberia for all I knew, but it was actually fifteen miles from Doncaster. We didn't make it in one day, but stayed overnight at The Reindeer Hotel in Barnby Moor. Next morning I wobbled along behind my parents and Pat, and we finally reached the Normanton Inn, right in the heart of Robin Hood country. We visited the Major Oak where Robin and his merry men did something, and paddled in Crackington Forge. The holiday lasted just three days, but in my mind we had been to an exotic foreign land. The Normanton Inn is now part of some ghastly restaurant chain, serving Sunday lunches on oval plates for £7.99, followed by a choice of Black Forest Gateau or Pear Belle Helene. On Mother's Day you can take grannie for a pound (and leave her there for two, hopefully).

In 1948, Father had a rather ambitious idea. He would take the family to Brittany, to a little town called Plougasnou on the north coast. We went with some friends of my parents, a doctor from Wakefield with two sons – very dishy boys as I remember – and at 14 and 17 respectively Pat and I ought to have been delighted, but as anyone of my generation knows, the opposite sex was a complete mystery to us.

France really wasn't geared up for tourism just three years after the war, and the Hotel de la Bain hadn't even managed to acquire any tablecloths. The en suite bathroom in those days was a shared basin in the corridor, with a blocked plughole. We drew lots for rooms, and Pat and I were lucky: we picked the room over the village toyshop, with an outside loo down the garden that stank of boiled turbot.

The staple diet on this holiday, I seem to remember, was artichokes. Never having seen one before, we all set about with a knife and fork to eat the entire thing; actually hunger probably drove us to it. The beach of course was totally inaccessible, with coils of barbed wire and notices about mines everywhere. We might as well have been a hundred miles inland.

I have a vivid memory of Mother pleading with Pat and me not to grumble about any aspect of the holiday because it would upset Father, who, she stressed, had paid a great deal of money for it. I'd love to know exactly how much it was. If it was a lot, he got astonishingly bad value for his money.

On the way home Mother had a blazing row with the other family, right in the middle of a very busy city. I don't know what the cause was, but we went our separate ways, never to see them again. It occurs to me, as I write, that Mother wasn't a woman to be trifled with, the word 'apology' simply not being part of her vocabulary.

In the middle of the war I was sent to the Convent Collegiate School in Doncaster. I made absolutely no impression there, and there are only two memories that I retain with any clarity. The first was when I was hit over the knuckles by a nun for using the wrong staircase; the second was when I stole a celluloid dwarf hanging on the lapel of a coat in the cloakroom. It had obviously come from a cracker, and wasn't worth a farthing, but I wanted it so badly, I took it.

Every time I went to the loo at the convent, I kissed the Virgin Mary's feet on her statue in the corridor, which gives you some idea of how indoctrinated we were by the nuns. Being C of E I had to sit at the back of the class during catechism lessons ("Who made you? God made me.") That's all I remember of the teaching, but I *do* remember being told that if we hadn't been baptised we would go to 'Limbo', which apparently entailed sitting on a concrete slab with no knickers on. In a panic, I asked Mother if I had been baptised, and in her usual casual manner she said that she didn't know – either Pat or I had been, in a kidney dish in the surgery, but she couldn't remember which of us it was. After telling this story to Father, he decided I should go to boarding school.

Choosing private schools for today's generation involves taking the children on inspection tours of shortlisted establishments, where they sample the school food, tour the science block, peruse the library, consider the stylishness of the uniform ("No way am I wearing those skirts/culottes/flares/that tie", "I want to wear my hear loose!") and make sure that the facilities meet their exacting requirements. No such consultation took place in my day. I wasn't aware what a boarding school involved, and there was no question of me visiting several in order to make a choice. Unbeknown to me, my parents travelled to Queen Margaret's, a Woodard school near York, and Mother simply said, "You'll love it darling, they wear long red cloaks".

And that was that.

Hoping for a reduction in the school fees, Father submitted me for the scholarship exam. Either he had blind faith in me, or it was his idea of a good joke. Latin was one of the papers, and as I hadn't done any at my previous school, I was given three weeks of private coaching immediately before the exam. On reading the paper I saw just one word which I knew, 'porto', so in the middle of completely blank sheets I put '7b) To carry'.

I didn't get the scholarship.

Chapter Two – Growing Up

My new seat of learning, Queen Margaret's School, was evacuated during the war to Castle Howard, the glorious Vanbrughian mansion situated in the North Yorkshire Wolds, after suffering a landmine attack on its original home in Scarborough. Had I been able to travel through time and see the BBC's *Brideshead Revisited* before being sent there for five years, I might have appreciated the priceless and truly beautiful works of art left *in situ* by the Howard family. As it was, neither I nor any of my fellow pupils had the slightest respect for any of the treasures. I well remember stuffing toffee paper up the nostrils of The Dying Gladiator, flicking ink pellets at the Gainsboroughs, and, most fun of all, inserting our penknives under the gold-embossed fruit on the wallpaper, in order to project it across the room. If only I had observed more closely the granite statues of Apollo and Zeus I would have at least made a start on my sex education. As it was, we were disgusted at having to eat our lunch next to a marble Romulus and Remus suckling from a hairy goat.

There was no heating of any kind in the building, save an enormous open log fire in the great hall, but that was out of bounds. The Castle suffered two very serious fires during the school's stay there – the Howard family must have been delighted to see the back of us in the fifties. The fires were not entirely our fault, but I bet it was the only time the girls felt any warmth. Needless to say, there was no hot water either, so at seven each morning we had to fetch a jug of icy water from the bathroom, and pour a dribble each into the ewers. Lack of heat was compounded, in the case of the lower forms, by lack of light. We had our lessons in the lower corridors which had virtually no daylight – we must have looked like forced rhubarb.

Pat and me at the Convent School in 1938.

As I wasn't academic, wasn't very good at music or drama, and was hopeless at sport, my time at Queen Margaret's was not very distinguished. On the academic side, the written word was a complete mystery to me, and still is to some extent. I turned in a particularly woeful performance in the English Literature mock school certificate exam, for which we had been studying a rather dull book called *A Shepherd's Life* by W.H. Hudson. I think it was a light depiction of life in rural Wiltshire, and in one of the chapters the author considered the paintings of Salisbury Cathedral by Turner and Constable. I didn't grasp the significance of this chapter, or more likely I couldn't be bothered to think about it; either way I was completely unprepared for the exam question which instructed candidates simply to "Compare the works of Constable and Turner".

Failing to see the word "and", I launched into a long dissertation extolling the virtues of Constable Turner, giving a graphic account of police life in Dorset. QM's headmistress, Miss Brown (known for her imperious air as 'Caesar'), viewed this slip-up unsympathetically, and took, to my mind, a sadistic delight in tearing up my paper in front of the entire class, much to their amusement. I admired this woman in a way, but my sister hated her and swore she would return to the school after leaving, pin her against a wall and beat her with a wire hairbrush! Caesar was heard to say one day that her favourite view in the land was King's Cross Station, from the north! What a snob. Sadly, she died of cancer soon after retirement.

Pat's dislike of Caesar had other root causes too. She was a keen and talented actress and was used to being given the leading role in school productions, but after being caught sliding down a drainpipe and tearing her navy blue knickers, was demoted from the leading role in 'Cavalcade' to being an off-stage seagull, sloshing a mop up and down in a bucket and squawking. This humiliation soured her relationship with Caesar irreparably.

Pat was far more worldly than I. When she left school she won a place at the Royal Academy of Music in London to study drama, and, after a good tight perm, was despatched in flat shoes and tweed suit to digs in Maida Vale.

I wasn't a sporty type either. In fact, I hated every minute of it. Standing in a field at eight o'clock on a frosty morning to catch cricket balls propelled at speed from a prefect's bat was not my idea of fun, especially with aching chilblains. There were thirty-four girls in our house, with places for thirty-three of them in the three teams of eleven. Guess who cut up the lemons at half-time? I didn't start my periods till I was nearly eighteen, but after noticing that my friends signed a little book every four weeks and magically got off games and gym, I signed it too, and it seemed to work.

In my seventy-odd years, I have never had my head under water. I swim vertically, legs dangling beneath me like shark bait, and consequently progress through the water is extremely slow. The only place we could swim at Castle Howard was in the fountain, the beautiful one so often depicted in photographs, with Atlas bearing the world on his shoulders. At its deepest point the water was two feet deep, it was crawling with little red worms, and it was slimy. Little wonder I didn't relish putting my head under. On visiting the school recently in its present location at Escrick Park, near York, I was shown their new Olympic-sized indoor pool, and was slightly aggrieved that all the donations that my father made to the school were squandered on altar frontals. We had a different coloured front for every day of the year. Why on earth couldn't they have spent a little of the money on a swimming pool?

Being an all-girls boarding school, Queen Margaret's was hardly the place to learn about the opposite sex. We were never told that there were two sexes and, to all intents and purposes, in our lives there was only one. School gossip did not revolve around boys, because we had no contact with them. We weren't even allowed to look out of the school gate in case we caught a glimpse of one, and our interest therefore centred around which mistress was in love with which other mistress. You either danced backwards or forwards, and when it came to drawing partners for the Christmas party I could never understand the consternation of the girls who drew the vicar, the doctor, or the gardener. Pat was just as naïve as I was. Once, while dancing with the six-foot tall violin teacher, she commented, "I suppose with you being so tall you always dance man?" I think her moustache added to Pat's confusion.

My school days are, in the main, very forgettable. I excelled at nothing, except perhaps needlework. I never made it into the main gang – that was for the sporty types, the form prefects who wore department badges on their tunics. For friends, I had to content myself with a few unremarkable underdogs: swots and girls with personality deficiencies. It is hilarious these days to attend school reunions, which is what one does in later life. There are usually a good number of my contemporaries at these "dos", many unmarried, all with hip or knee replacements, very few divorced, and all their children doing great works in far-off lands.

Five years went by at a sedate pace and eventually I found myself in the final term of the final year with my future looming – empty, uncharted, a blank canvas. Nowadays, girls leave school (the better ones, anyway) with ambitions, career plans, and life goals. In the early fifties, it was rare in the extreme for girls to set their sights on a career. Only three members of my class went to university; the majority had no ambitions at all. They just wanted to stay at home, help mother organise balls and shoots, and generally sit around waiting for a nice rich man, or even a nasty rich man, to marry them. As I prepared to leave, my horizons were narrow and hazy, and that's before you even consider my complete lack of talent.

The form was that each girl had an appointment with the headmistress in their last term to discuss their future. My turn came and I shuffled into Caesar's room. She peered over her pince-nez and enquired as she shook my hand, "And what, precisely do you intend to do in life Charlie", which is what comes out when one says Shirley with a plum in one's mouth. When I announced my intention to study art her reply was quite understandably, "Well I s'pose that's all you can do really".

I could hardly disagree. If anything it was a generous assessment.

You may well ask why on earth I wanted to do art in the first place. It was largely because all other options were unthinkable.

The idea of staying at home to help my mother around the house was ludicrous, since I had no aptitude in that sort of thing and we'd have driven each other mad. I was the only girl to ever receive 0% in a domestic science examination – slightly unfairly, I thought. I'm sure I spelt my name correctly on the paper. The practical exam required us to skin and casserole a rabbit, wash and iron the twenty-stone teacher's white overall, and produce six crisp pancakes in two and a half hours. I have an aversion to raw meat, especially in a fur jacket, and a serious fear of hot fat. My chum offered to undertake the skinning of my rabbit if I would do her vegetables, which was a fair exchange, I reckoned. The pancakes, however, would have to be all my own work. I was off sick the day they learned pancakes, but what the heck – it's a simple matter of frying flour and water.

Having mixed a good sturdy bowl of batter I put a pan of deep fat on a very low flame, so that it wouldn't overheat and burst into flames. As it became warm to the touch, I poured in a good inch of batter, and left it to get thoroughly 'cooked through', whilst I tackled the soaking wet overall – a task rather similar to pressing a marquee after a thunderstorm. A few minutes went by. I returned to the pancake, stout spatula in hand, turned it over, and went back to the overall. The one lesson I had learned was that presentation is everything, so to impress the examiner, I folded the wretched overall like it was on display in Next. I remember the examiner pressing it to her cheek, in order to detect any dampness. Mine nearly brought her hair out of curl.

The pancake was proving a little more difficult, and now resembled a queen-sized mattress. I heaved it out of the pan, dripping with fat, and plonked it on a paper doily, which was meant to soak up the excess grease. Unfortunately, the doily wasn't up to the task. In fact it was completely overwhelmed. In the dying moments before the arrival of the examiner I must have changed that pancake's nappy a dozen times. The plan was to roll it up and dust with sugar; I did well to force it over in the middle and pin it down it with a row of cocktail sticks.

So, any career to do with cooking or homemaking was out of the question. What else was there?

I've already mentioned that most of my contemporaries simply wanted to find a husband as quickly as possible and settle down to family life. This didn't appeal to me much, but even if it had, it was impossible for the very good reason that I was completely unable to attract a man of any description. Social life in sunny Doncaster at the beginning of the fifties was limited, as you'll appreciate if I tell you that the annual highlight was the Rotary Club Family Ball.

My chances of hitting it off with a man at this event were scuppered somewhat by Mother, who not only chose for me a sugar pink taffeta dress with puffed sleeves and a large bow across where my bosoms would have been had I had any, but insisted on regaling any prospective mate with details of my talents, my beauty, and my ultimate suitability to make him a ravishing wife. I am fairly certain that my mother was the character on whom Jane Austen modelled Mrs Bennet in *Pride and Prejudice*.

Then there was the annual Young Peoples Tea Dance, organised by three worthy mothers of other desperate daughters. Orange juice was the beverage of the evening, in plentiful supply, but there was a strict prohibition on alcohol. One year Pat invited a party of American music students and sneaked them over the road to the White Elephant pub for a quick pint. This must have been in about 1950. Mother received a telephone call the next day, and was told that Pat would be barred from any further Young Peoples Tea Dances. Lucky her, quite frankly.

Alcohol or no alcohol, I sat the entire evening with my back to the wall pretending to be transfixed by the musical quartet of ladies in long black dinner gowns. It was a relief to be able to slide off to collect my coat before the crush. Not that I was devoid of lust or romantic urges. More on that later.

In my bones, I felt that my future lay in doing something creative. I had always hankered after being an architect, but my School Certificate results put paid to that idea. So after pondering the options I applied to Sheffield Art College and Doncaster School of Art. By some fluke I got into both, but Mother considered Sheffield to be too far from home (twenty miles) and not a nice place for her daughter to be, so I had to settle for Doncaster, starting a four year course in 1951.

I didn't immediately specialise in textile design, but ended up doing it by default, after fairly dismal performances in art and pottery. The problem in art was not only that I lacked skill, but that I was quite unable to cope with the life classes. When confronted with a naked female model at my first life class, I cowered behind my easel for a good ten minutes, and then, having plucked up the courage to peep over the top, grasped the charcoal and with sweating hand traced a thick black line round the edge of her extraordinary form, hoping that when I got back to the starting point it would meet up! The thought of having to do this every week was too much.

My pottery classes were no better. For some reason, I was made demonstrator on the wheel on Open Day. I hadn't quite mastered the technique of slicing a pot off the wheel with the cheese cutter, so instead of producing a shapely vase I diced off a line of rather ordinary napkin rings. (In the North we always refer to these as serviette rings, but since my children went south to SW11 I've been told 'serviette' is common.)

After the first two years in which we had to study every aspect of art, calligraphy, heraldry, history of art, architecture, pottery, oil painting, life drawing, weaving and textile design, we had to specialise in two of these for our final NDD (National Diploma in Design) exam.* I chose the textile course and weaving.

The other major gap in my knowledge – the opposite sex – improved slightly in my student years. Not on the physical front, but at least at Doncaster I was in the vicinity of boys. I fell madly in love with one of them, called Geoffrey. He wore royal blue cords, fur gloves, had long curly hair cascading onto his shoulders, and was very handsome by any standard, but he slept with his mother. I was once invited to ride home on the back of a tandem bicycle by a lad called Clarkson (no relation) and as we reached my gate he asked me to go to the cinema with him. I immediately panicked, said "No", and learned the next day that he had asked my best friend instead.

My only true date was with a very wealthy, highly intellectual young man, a sort of scholarship-to-Harvard type, called Simon. I suspect the evening had been arranged by his mother, who obviously considered the local doctor's daughter a good catch. We went to see *King Kong* at the Ritz Cinema. Simon had a very bad cold, he hadn't mastered the art

---

*Years later, when Eddie and I were trying to persuade the Council to let us open a nursery school in Doncaster, and they asked what qualifications I had, I referred them to my 'NDD' and claimed it was a Nursing Diploma. They were impressed, but the idea never came to fruition, mainly because our intended partner in the enterprise was a lady who didn't agree to the children using paint, Plasticine, sand, water or clay. When I tell you that she would only allow the doctor to examine her through an eiderdown, it was perhaps a good thing that we didn't form a partnership.

of driving a motor vehicle as yet, so we went back to his house on the bus. His mother had prepared a nice supper for us which included green jelly and lashings of hot chocolate. Simon retired to bed to nurse his cold, and his father ran me home, as it was nearing eleven o'clock, and no time for a young maiden to still be up! Joining my father in a whisky, he proceeded to itemise his son's many talents and announced that, "Simon was looking to feather his nest". Not with me he wasn't!

I don't think I was either particularly good or particularly bad at textile design, but by my fourth year at Doncaster School of Art it was clear that I wasn't going to *be* a textile designer, or any other kind of artist for that matter.

I spent a few miserable days trailing my portfolio around Lancashire, but the only job offer I received was at a bedding factory in Blackburn helping to design mattress ticking! Most people think of mattresses as being black and white stripes, but in Blackburn they favour damask chrysanthemums. I turned down the mattress offer and related this to a colleague, who immediately secured the job for herself and promptly married the managing director. I hope she was happy!

To the astonishment of my tutors and fellow pupils, I was invited to apply for a place at the Royal College of Art in London. To their even greater astonishment, on the strength of my application I was asked for an interview. Off I went, wildly excited at the prospect of three days in the great metropolis alone.

My only other visits to London had been in my father's Bentley, as a child, when the one hundred and sixty mile trip would take a good two days, especially if the level crossing gates were closed at Ranby on the A1. On those trips, we couldn't make London in one day, so we stopped for coffee in Stamford, and had a picnic lunch in a country lane just outside Grantham. That's where the car sickness pills were secreted into my egg sandwiches, because we'd already had to stop four times for me to throw up. Tea was taken in Buckden at The George and a few hours later we would pull into the George and Dragon in Baldock for the night. If we made an early start the next morning we could make London by lunchtime. We always stayed in the hotel above Quaglinos Restaurant (I think it was called 'Maurice'), had our hair coiffured at French's in Half Moon Street, and visited the theatre at least half a dozen times in the five days. Although I was only young at the time, these trips were definitely the inspiration for my love of theatre which has remained with me all my life. We saw Laurence Olivier in *The Sleeping Prince* but my favourite play was *The Winslow Boy*, in which we saw the great Robert Donat. I get a real pang of nostalgia when I hear those immortal words "Let right be done". My father's devotion to Gilbert and Sullivan meant we had to include whatever was showing at The Savoy Theatre at the time. I always came home starry-eyed, and spent the next few months listening to his collection of 78s, and trying to write the words down. Had I known we had a book of G and S lyrics in the house, it would have saved all that endless changing of the needles.

This trip to London was different, I was alone, footloose, and sex-starved! The interview at the Royal College was excruciatingly embarrassing. I only remember one question.

"Who is your favourite furniture designer?" I was asked.

I was relieved to be able to name one.

"Gordon Russell."

"And how do you think he compares with others?"

"Pretty well."

Even as I answered, I could feel my armpits becoming increasingly damp.

On the second day of the interview, we had a design exam. We were asked to create a curtain fabric for the conference suite of a zoo. I can picture my creation now, and still go hot and cold with embarrassment. Lime green pigeons eating navy blue corn!

I left at about five o'clock, not feeling overconfident of securing a place at the College, but excited at the prospect of a night alone "on the town". In a street just off the Cromwell Road there was, and still is I think, a little café. My evening of unbridled debauchery would start there with a cup of tea!

Seated at the next table was the man of my dreams. I hadn't seen such an Adonis since a skiing holiday in Switzerland at the age of fifteen when my instructor was a young man called Gabriel whose chronic conjunctivitis gave him an agreeably lascivious look as he peered through sore red eyes! Back in the café, I was conscious of being watched, a totally new experience for me, but had no idea why.

Finishing my cup of tea, I joined the bus queue on the Cromwell Road, when who should come around the corner but the man from the café! He was driving a low red sports car, probably a Ferrari, and wearing a duffle coat like the one worn by Jack Hawkins in *The Cruel Sea*. By this time it was starting to drizzle, so when he pulled up and offered me a lift in his strong foreign accent, what could be more natural than to hop in! I remember being very impressed with the kindness of London men. We chatted about this and that, and he asked what I was doing in London. I have a feeling that my tight Yorkshire perm, designed 'to last', coupled with a glimpse of my navy blue knickers, probably saved my life. He drove me to the door of my hotel, jumped out, kissed my hand, clicked his heels, said what a pleasure it had been to meet me, and escorted me to the door! So there.

At this time, I did know *where* babies came from, I just didn't know *how* it happened. My father had books in his study and. one day being confined to bed in that room, I found myself idly thumbing through a few – looking at the pictures at any rate – when I came across a thin red book entitled *Love and Marriage* by Marie Stopes. The diagrams were amazing! Surely that's not how it happens! I had once overheard Mother gossiping to a friend about a local girl, who was pregnant. Not only was this girl unmarried, but apparently she didn't know who the father was. Now if the diagrams in that book were correct, which frankly I doubted, how could that happen to a girl without her knowing? Perhaps it was dark, and she never saw his face?

I was eighteen for God's sake.

I arrived back home after the interview in London, still a very bright shade of green, with my future still undecided. Needless to say, the Royal College didn't offer me a place, so I returned to Doncaster to finish my course. To give me something to do, and thinking it might advance my social life, I enrolled in the local amateur operatic society. Not being able to sing, I was naturally confined to the chorus, usually the back row. In a production of *Iolanthe* I was a member of the fairy chorus! Gilbert and Sullivan fans will be familiar with the "tripping hither, tripping thither" sequence. Dressed in white tutus and carrying silver wands six feet long with a star on the end, we massed in the wings ready for our entrance. Stupidly, seeing a knot-hole in the boards I couldn't resist the temptation to poke my wand down it. The wag of an Assistant Stage Manager underneath also couldn't resist the temptation to pull it. The orchestra struck up and on we trouped, fifteen members of the chorus waving their long wands and me with a silver star stuck on my thumb.

The highlight of my amateur dramatic career came at the age of seventeen when I was given a part in the Thespian Society's production of Ivor Novello's *The Dancing Years*. This was to be staged at the Gaumont Palace Cinema in Doncaster, with an audience of over two thousand. Not only did I have to sing, but also dance, neither of which I could do. I was Greta, the young lead, who was madly in love with Rudi. Rudi's part was given to a new member of the society, an ex-professional, rather dishy, albeit raddled, middle-aged man in his fifties. He had definitely "seen life" but was now running a DIY shop on the high street. I had to go to an upstairs room above his shop for rehearsals, and – horror of horrors – I had to kiss him. The show was a sell-out. I warbled my way through my solo Primrose, danced my ballet sequence with Bill, a shoe shop assistant, and received rave notices. In provincial towns, in those days, the theatre critic was usually a friend of the family, in my case probably a patient of my father's, and they wouldn't dare upset you.

Time went by. Although Mother was hoping as every day passed that I would find a suitable man to marry, I began to think that maybe I should get a job. The subject was never discussed, and when I consider how much pressure is put upon youngsters today to sort out their careers, maybe I was lucky. I have no recollection of how I managed to secure employment. I had definitely never heard of the *Times Educational Supplement*, but I must have somehow wandered into an Education Office somewhere and offered my services. Again, I have no idea where I heard about a vacancy for an occupational therapist, I didn't even know what one was, but I went along for an interview at Rotherham Moorgate Hospital, the most grim, forbidding place you could ever imagine.

I had a chat with a charming white-haired doctor, who seemed to like me, so I got the job. There was a tiny little room, in which stood a cupboard full of lampshade frames, felt squares, embroidery silks, a wonderful plastic-type sheeting called crinothene, and one or two little looms. I bought a paper pattern of a felt rabbit holding a carrot, and after cutting out the pieces, set off around the various wards, distributing these to some rather surprised and unenthusiastic patients. As it was a part-time job of about one and a half days a week, by the time of my second visit most of the original patients had been discharged. Somewhere in Rotherham there must be a cache of half stuffed rabbits.

In the mental ward, however, I had a permanent and captive audience. Most patients were in high-sided cots, through which it was difficult to pass lampshade frames. I had to cut the panels for the shades out of the crinothene, and with enormous difficulty punch holes around the edge of each panel, then I could deliver each patient a ball of thread and instructions on sewing the panels on to the frame. The patients were still there the following week, but when I returned there was never any sign of the thread, or indeed the crinothene. The lampshade frames were mostly found under the beds, but the rest they had either eaten, or the nurse had removed the thread before they throttled themselves with it.

Word of my achievements must have spread, because shortly afterwards I got another day a week at a hospital for T.B. sufferers in Mexborough. They all wanted to make housecoats – not easy.

Alongside these jobs, I was employed to teach infants in a little church school in Harworth, the colliery village in North Nottinghamshire. There were just three other teachers, the headmaster, Mr B. a chain smoker, who always had a dirty collar, and a very fat spinster whom the headmaster was alleged to be "seeing". The Head and his mistress both had coal fires in their classrooms, but they told me that I wasn't entitled to a fire because I hadn't been teaching long enough! Imagine telling a young teacher that today, and her accepting it. The NUT would call a national strike.

The staff room at the school was in the potting shed. It was across the yard, and was full of sacks of potatoes, one of which was my seat. Presumably I hadn't been teaching long enough to be indulged with a chair. Before lunch, a little child would carry in an enamel bowl of warm water in which we all washed our hands in turn. I came last. Mr B. always washed his face in the bowl, and finished with a spit. Then it was my turn!

The only upside to this miserable initiation in teaching was the fact that all three jobs were in different authorities: one hospital in Rotherham, South Yorkshire; another hospital in Mexborough in the Don Valley; and a school in Harworth, Nottinghamshire. No one ever cottoned on to me being the same person, so the nine pounds I earned came entirely tax-free.

Chapter Three – Eddie

Slowly, my social life picked up. Every town in Britain has a tennis club, and in the fifties they were a great place to meet "the man". I joined the Doncaster club and did. He was devastatingly handsome, so consequently always sported a beautiful blonde on one arm. Never mind – one virtue I do admit to possessing is dogged determination, I bided my time and we were married in 1957.

Eddie was quite extraordinary. His parents owned a pub in Tickhill, a charming little village south of Doncaster. Having suffered appalling asthma all his young life, he had barely had any education. Leaving school at 14 and considered to be the black sheep of the family, he struggled to make his way in the world. His four sisters and brothers all married local boys/girls, all had jobs locally, and conformed. Eddie didn't.

He started work for 7s 6p a week in the local builders yard, but very quickly realised this was not for him, so became a salesman for a firm of timber merchants and would have done quite well there if he hadn't wrapped his boss's car round a tree in the first week. There followed a series of similar selling jobs in the building industry, most of which ended in an accident of some kind!

He then joined the Doncaster Tennis Club, much to the annoyance of his parents who considered Tickhill Tennis Club quite good enough. When he started "seeing" a doctor's daughter from the other side of Doncaster, and parking her father's Bentley in the pub yard for the night, they realised there was no hope for him. I think it says so much about my Father's character that one night after Eddie missed his last bus to Tickhill, he was given the Bentley to take home. Not only that, but Pat's boyfriend had also missed his last bus, so he was given Mother's Morris Minor. When the usual night call came through, Father, finding the garage devoid of cars, took to his bicycle. The only comment he made at breakfast was, "Did you both have a good time last night?"

After about three months Eddie finally plucked up the courage to invite me to the pictures. Can you believe that I actually went home from school at lunchtime to have a bath and starch the *broidery Anglaise* frill on my underskirt? We didn't actually make bodily contact – well, he probably couldn't get past the starch – for at least the first few dates, and as for a kiss, I reckon it must have been 6 months at least.

He finally secured a very good job in Stourbridge, near Birmingham, living in digs. He had bought a 1930s Austin 7 sports car with borrowed money – and bald tyres – and raced up to Doncaster at weekends to see me. They were beautiful times, innocent fun, parties on orange juice, tennis, and amateur dramatics. Eddie finally borrowed enough money, £35, from his dad to buy me an engagement ring, and we were married in August 1957.

Eddie was renowned for his sartorial appearance. He was fanatical about his dress – his trousers were pressed daily. In his early days as a salesman, he had to have a clean white shirt, a starched collar and cuffs, a silk tie and only the most expensive leather shoes, regardless of his financial circumstances.

With the help of my father, we managed to purchase a tiny two-bedroomed cottage in Sprotborough as our first home. It cost him £900, and in the process of converting it, our manic love of old property developed.

I was only 22 and early married life is never easy, but when you marry an accident-prone, 24 year-old, mad car nut, it's damn near impossible. A month before our wedding, he once again wrapped his boss's car around a bus stop, breaking a number of bones and ending up in Doncaster Royal Infirmary, which in those days was a forbidding, Dickensian institution. Separate from the main grim building were a number of even grimmer wooden huts. They had been erected hurriedly during the war to accommodate wounded soldiers, and were never demolished. One of these was Eddie's ward. In the middle of the hut, which housed about twenty beds, was a large coke stove, belching out fumes. The linoleum floor was pitted with holes, and the bed linen was grey, stained and ragged. Eddie's mother insisted on taking it home for a good boiling! Having owned a pub for many years, I think she probably had what today would be called OCD – Obsessive Cleaning Disorder. She washed and starched her antimacassars every Monday whether or not anyone had entered the sitting room all week, and was the only woman I ever knew who took a nail file to the bottoms of chair legs.

The Ward Sister, a fearsome woman with a face like a bulldog chewing a wasp, said as I entered the hut, "There'll be no wedding for you my dear, your fiancée's broken his neck". Not the best of bedside manners, but at least the nurses all wore starched white aprons and called you Mrs Clarkson. Many years later, in one of Eddie's later hospitals, a nurse of about twelve perched on his bed and said, "I'm Linda, and what shall I call you?"

"You can call me Mr Clarkson, and I shall call you Staff Nurse," he replied. That's my Eddie.

I spent my honeymoon night sitting up in bed, finishing off a fisherman's rib double-knit sweater. Well what else can you do when your partner is encased in plaster of Paris from elbow to ankle? Huge joke captions accompanied our wedding photographs in the local press: "Groom plastered before the wedding starts", "Old boot on foot not on car", etc.

We missed the plane from Manchester to Dublin, but the airline took pity on us and managed to squeeze us on a flight that had stopped over from Frankfurt on its way to Ireland. At Dublin, we hired a Volkswagen Beetle, which was far too small and meant that Eddie had to lie in the back seat with his various broken limbs stretched out around the car. We drove across to Parknasilla, an idyllic part of Southern Ireland situated on an estuary of breathtaking beauty. Sexual pleasures were not high on the agenda, but it's amazing how these can be replaced by staggering vistas of mountains and lakes.

Little did we know, but the motoring accident a month before we married would seem like a playground graze compared to the five that followed soon afterwards. Telegraph poles, brewery wagons, roundabouts, and flights of concrete steps all made contact with one or many of Eddie's bones. The month after we were married, he met a brewery lorry on a humpback bridge in thick fog. He crawled from the mangled wreck of his car, walked to the local doctor's house and asked the doctor's wife if she would kindly ring my father and tell him that his son-in-law would be popping in to the infirmary for a check-up. By the time I arrived, he was having his smashed patella removed, along with most of his teeth. In all, Eddie had three patellas removed. I know, the human frame only has two, but Eddie's body was different to anything medical science had seen before. He always said that when he died they would keep his body in a cupboard, and bring it out on Friday afternoons when medical students had had a hard week, so that they could enjoy a good laugh.

Considering the unbroken succession of Eddie's injuries, it is maybe surprising that in 1960 Jeremy was born and two years later was followed by Joanna. When I first became pregnant I was just overjoyed to learn that there was a baby in there. So delighted in fact that I rushed down to announce it to my parents, two hours after my period was late. (I always started before the nine o'clock news, and the epilogue had started!)

My ever-cautious, wise father, asked how late I was, and feeling rather ashamed to say anything less, I lied, saying it was three weeks. "That's far too early to get excited," he said. "Wait another month or so."

My first pregnancy was a nightmare. I knew so little about the whole ghastly business. There were no antenatal clinics in those days, and no district nurses on hand to answer all the queries that newly-pregnant women have. I was violently sick for the entire nine months. Father reluctantly agreed that maybe I should take some tablets for it, and prescribed one of the two new anti-nausea drugs on the market at the time. One of these was Thalidomide. I took the other one.

The tablets did me little good. I never dressed, but just rolled around in my dressing gown, groaning all day. I couldn't bear the smell of the new pink Kosset carpet in our bedroom, or the sight of a chocolate digestive biscuit.

Jeremy was due on the 24th March at 9.30pm, so by the second week in April I was getting somewhat impatient. Father popped his head round the door every day after morning surgery and enquired if anything had happened yet. As if I had any idea what should have happened! I was booked to have the baby at a nursing home in Doncaster, a large semi-detached three-storey building with no lift, run by an overweight Scottish lady named Mrs Farrar. Suffering a mild bout of indigestion in the middle of the night, I decided this must be it. Eddie rushed me in to the nursing home, and there I lay for about four days, doing nothing. It was a cosy affair. Mr Farrar came up each evening with his sherry to sit on the bed for a chat. I remember the trays on which meals were served, plywood with a wicker rail around the edge, the sort made by the blind. Unfortunately, not ideal for removing pieces of dried scrambled egg.

While I was safely out of the way, Eddie planned to paint the entire outside walls of our cottage as a surprise for me when I came home, so he didn't really have time to visit me very much. Mother came all too regularly, now in the early stages of her mental illness.

I was finally moved to what was laughingly called the labour ward, a tiny bare room, with dirty windows, and the hardest bed you could imagine. By this time I was in extreme pain; my waters had broken, which was a shock, because no one had told me about that delight. Eventually the gynaecologist visited me, and I overheard her telling Mrs Farrar something about the baby being in distress, and *quick quick, call the surgeon*. Honestly and truly, I did not know what a caesarean was.

Eddie and Mother had taken to the sherry bottle in a big way, and when they arrived, Eddie immediately fainted on the landing. As he hit the linoleum floor, I was being transported in a canvas bag down to the basement which housed the operating theatre. The staircase was so narrow and winding that a stretcher was useless. Seeing a prostrate Eddie, the volunteers put me down on the floor, and carried him to my bed, where there was lots of loosening of his collar and requests for brandy. When they had made him comfortable, they returned to me, picked me off the floor, and I continued my journey down the last flight of stairs. I don't think caesarean scars today stretch from your throat downwards, but I have to wear high-necked jumpers.

When I miraculously became pregnant a second time, I booked in for the operation to suit the surgeon's holiday commitments, and things were not quite so dramatic. I think anyone having the same experiences today would not only sue the NHS, but it would make headlines in *The Sun*. We were so naïve and trusting about things in those days, especially when it came to professionals like doctors.

Eddie was a brilliant salesman, and in our early years of marriage in the sixties he was working for a firm of building suppliers. I was having difficulty holding down any job, due to the fact that every five minutes I had to give it up and drive him around the country, but I did do some part-time teaching. We were totally irresponsible, incapable of setting an alarm clock, and one morning awoke to the sound of little children skipping down the road to the village school. In a panic we jumped out of bed thinking it must be nearly nine o'clock, and found to our horror that they were returning to school after lunch!

The school in which I taught at that time had a completely eccentric headmistress. She was dirty, and her underskirt always hung six inches below her dress. She knew I had been to art school, and would rush into my classroom, in which I was attempting to teach forty eight-year-olds, and deposit a bundle of old newspapers on my desk, demanding a life-sized *papier maché* model of a camel in the main entrance, before four o'clock.

After Joanna was born in 1962 we realised we needed somewhere larger than our cottage, and our eye was caught by an enormous, derelict farmhouse, in a tiny hamlet just north of Doncaster. It was not on the market, but we knew the farmer who owned it and managed to beat him down from £1,500 to £1,000. It was called 'Home Farm' and was in a pretty hamlet with the wonderful name of Burghwallis.

Home Farm's walls were encrusted with thick green moss – and that was on the inside. The roof had collapsed years earlier, and the rafters played host to a display of rose-bay willow herb. Local lads had used the attic as a bonfire site, and, worst of all, the outgoing farm tenants had painted the stone mullion windows with thick gloss red paint.

Undaunted, we borrowed huge amounts from the bank manager, a man who was known to be very intolerant of late mortgage repayments. In the years after we bought Home Farm, when money was tight, Eddie would often enter the bank on hands and knees and present his cheque for cash withdrawal without daring to poke his head over the top of the counter. It was amazing how often the cashier would identify him just by his hand, and leaning over the counter would announce "Mr Robson would like to see you Mr Clarkson".

Asked to account for our awful finances, Eddie would say that he was just about to get an insurance payment for his most recent personal injury, and that was usually enough to keep Mr Robson quiet for a while longer. When insurance payments came in, Mr Robson, of course, never got a whiff of them, because by that time the carpet fitter would be screaming for payment. Like many families with young children, it was hard making ends meet. Every Tuesday morning I would stand on the steps of the post office, waiting for it to open, so that I could collect my eight shillings family allowance. Without that, there was no bread on the table.

There was no question of hiring professional decorators for Home Farm, so our evenings were spent hacking off damp plaster, sanding whitewash from the oak beams which ran the entire length of the house, and removing thick scarlet gloss paint from the stone mullions. The paint removal had to be done with copper discs on electric drills and, even with surgical masks on, Eddie's and my lungs felt as if they were caked with ground paint dust.

Everybody can remember where they were in November 1963 when they heard that President Kennedy had been assassinated. We were working on the sitting room beams, wearing plastic bath hats, motorcycle goggles, surgical masks, and rubber gloves. Needing a certain tool, I slipped across the road to a friend's house to ask if they had one, wearing the full rig, and with a half-inch layer of woodworm dust over me. My friend's wife opened the door with tears streaming down her face, clutched me to her bosom, and sobbed, "He's dead". It took a while to realise she didn't mean her husband. After her divorce, she rather wished it had been.

We couldn't afford plaster for our refurbishment, but found a wonderful substitute called Frestex, which we slopped over the walls with a tar brush. It dried, and was ready to paint in twenty-four hours. Sadly, Frestex has been taken off the market – must have been something to do with the Plasterers Union. The garden of Home Farm was, needless to say, a jungle, with piles of rubble here and there, which, together with discarded cardboard boxes, made a wonderful play area for the children.

Our finances finally reached crisis point when, to Mr Robson's chagrin, we entered Jeremy at the local prep school, never giving a thought as to where we would find the sixty-seven pounds for the first term's fees. There was but one solution: I had to change from being a part-time teacher to a full-time one, and bring in more money.

In the mid sixties teachers were in short supply, and schools were grateful for anyone who could stand, speak English, and keep forty five-year-olds in the same room for any length of time. They also would gladly find a place at nursery school for one's children.

I took a job at a school in a suburb of Doncaster called Hexthorpe and poor little Joanna was packed off to nursery at the age of two. I cried so much the first day I left her that I was incapable of teaching and spent the whole morning being consoled by the headmistress with cups of coffee. I can well understand the guilt of mothers today who are forced to leave their babies at school in order to go out and work.

I was by a long chalk the worst infant teacher in South Yorkshire. I knew I was bad at the job. I seemed incapable of progressing my eight year olds beyond page three of *Janet and John*. After nine months in my class, little David Smith was still wrestling daily with "Look, look an aeroplane". He's now probably working for air traffic control. Michael Shaw was so terrified of me, with good reason, that he nervously ate his wax crayons every morning. My favourite pupil, dear little Alan Scorer, was what today would be called a 'special needs' child, but in those days the term was 'educationally subnormal' or 'ESN'. When I last heard of Alan he was serving a long prison term for aggravated burglary, following a four-year stretch for arson, having burned down the local comprehensive school. I should have seen it coming: his mother kept telling me he stuffed comics down his bed and set fire to them, and whenever I felt strong enough to embark on a painting session, Alan always depicted large red fire engines. What a tragedy the education psychologists didn't spot his potential as a budding fireman.

Although I was the wrong person in the wrong job, and although the school was in the slums of Doncaster, I loved teaching there. The kids were so deprived and neglected, they appreciated every little scrap of attention and love you could give them. I'll never forget little Carol. Her Mum "worked nights", so she was never short of velvet and lace dresses, but she slept on the sofa every night with "Uncle Fred", and would be found by the caretaker sitting on the school steps at six o'clock every morning with a slice of jam and bread. A quick cuddle with her usually left me with nits.

It was around this time that my mother's illness became much more serious. Her heart condition was causing a series of minor strokes, which manifested themselves in paralysis of various limbs. These usually recovered, but when she lost her speech, that was permanent. It got to the point where she could say only one word – "Rossington" – inexplicable, because Rossington was a mining village south of Doncaster with which we had no connection whatsoever. The sad thing was, she believed she was talking normally, and the frustration it caused her was horrific.

Coupled with this, she had chronic manic depression. Three weeks of total inertia, bed-ridden, doubly-incontinent, was followed by three weeks of manic behaviour, staying up all night, cooking, washing, and most worrying of all, picking the babies from their cots! Eddie and I had moved into the family home, to enable Father to continue practising, as he was far too young to retire. He slept with the car keys around his neck, but to no avail. Mother cut them loose one night, and headed off in the Morris Minor. Missing for five hours, we feared the worst when we received a call from Pat, then living in Windsor. Mother had, it transpired, driven through the night and morning rush hour to Pat's, trading in the car's spare wheel for petrol along the way. Uttering a string of "Rossingtons", she left the garage owner completely bemused and compounded his misery by demolishing a low brick wall as she left.

On another occasion, she refused to come home from town with me in the car, and locked herself in the garden privy of a stranger's cottage. Wearing a large brimmed velvet hat, and with her devoted corgi running back and forth, she popped her head over the door every few moments and shouted "Rossington!" at the astonished cottage owner.

I seemed to spend my days rushing around with the two babies in the car endlessly searching for her. I usually found her in town merrily shoplifting, but as she was well known in Doncaster, shopkeepers were very understanding. The owner of the high-class ladies gown shop, *Lucille*, was exceptionally good about it, and let Mother sit in the shop by the fire with a glass of sherry. She only drew the line when Mother blew raspberries at customers as they emerged from the changing rooms to indicate that she thought they looked ghastly.

A full-time nurse was employed, but as we welcomed her with a cup of tea, Mother ran upstairs and emptied her suitcase out of the bedroom window. Being a windy day, it took Pat and me hours to retrieve the lady's corsets from the rose bushes. A new housekeeper had a freshly-baked cream cake pressed into her face. One way or another, Mother made it very clear that she did not want any hired help.

Father was endlessly patient, and most days took my mother out on his rounds. She was desperate to take the wheel, and one day in a fit of pique threw the ignition key out of the window of the Bentley, then, while Father searched the grass verge, took off all her clothes. That took some explaining to the police.

They were difficult times.

Chapter Four – My French Connection

Whilst holidaying in France with friends – or rather, while enduring torture on a campsite – in 1967, we were idly gazing into gift shop windows wondering if my mother had any shelf space for yet another plastic Breton doll, when one of my friends, Jill, remarked, "Good God, Shirley, you could make everything in that shop window for tuppence!" That chance remark changed our lives. The seed of an idea was planted in my mind, and I couldn't wait to pack up the two soggy children, and an even soggier tent, and head for home.

Holidaying with friends, however much you love them, is a delicate balancing act, and this particular holiday had been more wobbly than usual. The scene was set when we arrived in France and I flatly refused to use a French lavatory. Brian, husband of Jill, made it quite clear he thought me unreasonable; only later, when he was forced to use 'the crouchers' himself, did he find it necessary to apologise. But the real problem was the weather, and our complete lack of preparation for it.

One unarguable fact was learned on that holiday: we are not as good at camping as the Germans. Before the holiday, Brian and Jill had bought a new tent at a knockdown price – I seem to remember the figure of £24 – but in their zeal for a bargain had overlooked a crucial fact: it had no waterproofing. This was a grave error. We all travelled overnight to the tiny island, Île de Ré, off the west coast of France, only to find, after this marathon driving stint, that the island was not only full, but was being buffeted by gales which had blown the campsite into the sea. Tired, and with jangled nerves, we headed back up the coast to Les Sables d'Olonne. Suffering the effects of the Benzedrine tablets that my father had prescribed to keep us awake, our judgement was somewhat impaired, and we pitched our tents in a lovely little hollow – well, the rest of the campsite was full to bursting, and this hollow was completely empty.

Whilst the sun shone, we were fine, and amazed our German neighbours by playing 'What's the time Mr Wolf?' and 'Grandmothers footsteps' with the children, completely ignoring the forecasts of bad weather. When the skies turned grey, the Germans produced an extraordinary collection of trenching tools from their car boots and set to work, digging deep moats around their tents. We thought they were mad, and headed for a fun-packed day on the beach.

The storm that duly arrived was indeed phenomenal, and we had to race for cover to the nearest café. With hindsight we should have raced back to the campsite to prevent the complete demolition of Brian and Jill's tent. The sight that greeted us on our return was hysterical: rows of silent Germans, arms folded, grim faced, muttering (I think), "That will take the silly smiles off their English faces". Their expertly dug trenches were performing exactly as designed, channelling the rainwater away from their tents … directly into our hollow. A bit mean we thought.

Brian and Jill's cheap tent was drenched and resembled a large wet handkerchief hanging limply over a twisted tangle of tubular framing. To make matters worse, that morning I had suggested to Brian that the space between the roof of the sleeping compartment and the outer canvas was a useful place to store clothing etc. No one had ever explained to me about capillary attraction.

With tears of laughter running down our faces, we tried wringing out the loo rolls, and drying sleeping bags over a primus stove. All to no avail. After another storm of equal ferocity we gave up the struggle, and all moved lock, stock and barrel into our tent, which hadn't suffered quite the same damage, although the awning poles had been flung like javelins three hundred yards across the campsite. Eight people in a tent designed for four had certain drawbacks, but on the brighter side, the worry of Jill forgetting her contraceptive pills was negated, though her bouts of diarrhoea throughout the night were a problem. (On arriving home Jill was in fact pregnant, and we all swear to this day that it must have been Dan, Dan, the Lavatory Man, who came at midnight to give "the crouchers" a good flushing out.)

Before the storm, it had been incredibly hot, and both Eddie and Brian had stupidly removed their socks – something men rarely do because their delicate, pale feet cannot stand the sun. Sure enough, for the next four days, they had to sit with their feet in canvas buckets, which we kept filling with sea water. They complained that the only way they could cope with the pain, was to drink copious quantities of wine and brandy. The car boots became so full of empties that Jill and I foolishly suggested that they go and return them, not realising that with both cars away, we had no power. After cooking supper for the four children and putting them to bed, in the dark, we waited for the men to return with the rain lashing our tent. They eventually pitched up at one in the morning, having consumed the proceeds of their bottle money. However they could no longer feel their feet, so that was good!

The journey home from this holiday was horrendous. Even though a Force 9 gale was blowing in the Channel, we defiantly headed off to the smorgasbord and ordered a three-course lunch, with a few bottles of wine. As we pulled out of Cherbourg, or Calais, or Dieppe – can't remember which, but I suspect it was Cherbourg because I know the journey lasted a week – we watched Joanna turn bright green, and before we could get to the loos she upchucked. We had no clean dry clothes, so I wrapped her in a large, damp, sand-filled towel, laid her on a bench, and went to retrieve Jeremy from the gents where he too was talking on the great white telephone.

Our friends too had succumbed, despite their protestations that they could weather any storm, and Jill was asleep with her face in a bowl of trifle. I remember seeing a vicar lying flat out on the deck in a pool of vomit, still clutching an open bible.

I purchased the last remaining box of Kleenex from the shop, mopped up most of E Deck and went to find Eddie. There he was, still sitting at the table, napkin tucked in his dirty t-shirt, pouring the last dregs of the Beaujolais into his glass. He had demolished four plates of lobster, and enjoyed most of the Brie. The big smile was quickly wiped off his face, I can tell you.

That holiday was fairly disastrous, but compared to a later one with yet more long-suffering friends, it was paradise. We were in Brittany in about 1970 when, during a scramble over the rocks on our first day, Eddie shouted to the children, "Take care on these rocks, they are very slippery". Before the words left his mouth, he went down like a poleaxed bull, and in trying to save himself put his hand out on a rock encrusted with razor-sharp shells. Most of the week was spent making trips to Auray, a small local town which boasted a magnificent hospital, due to the fact that the Minister of Health lived there. Hours of poking about with scalpels failed to detect the reason for Eddie's high temperature or for the large swelling under his arm. Red lines were running up and down his forearm, and it was evident that he was seriously ill. *Once again.*

Language problems made matters worse. Tony, our lifelong friend and lawyer, spoke passable French, but he kept fainting so was no use at all. Alarmingly, the word *ampute* kept cropping up in the conversation between doctors, and even we understood what that meant. Eddie was now virtually unconscious. It was clear that we had to head for home, and fast.

I had to drive the brand new car, which unknown to us had been supplied with a serious leak in the oil sump, up the M1 and straight to Doncaster Infirmary, where the chief consultant surgeon, a personal friend, whizzed him into the operating theatre via the X-ray department. To our great relief and his eternal amusement, he removed a large winkle shell (minus winkle) from Eddie's hand. An X-ray had never crossed the minds of the French doctors. Our friendly surgeon had a wicked sense of humour, and when he had stitched up Eddie's hand, but before he came round, he sent his houseman down to the fish market in the town to buy a plate of whelks, which he placed on the bedside table, claiming he had removed the lot.

The car was not so easily mended. The high-speed journey home minus oil had taken its toll. It sounded like a can of marbles as I drove it into the drive, it spluttered to a halt, with something called a 'big-end' gone. Our lovely new Ford Cortina was ignominiously hauled away on to a low-loader, never to be seen again.

So much for French holidays. The important thing about the first one was Jill's offhand remark about starting a business of my own, which had really got me thinking. Within a few days of arriving home, I rushed out to the local haberdashery to buy pieces of chipboard, gingham, glue, brass knobs, artificial flowery things, etc. etc. and set about hammering, gluing, and generally making some rather hideous little objects. This was in September 1967, so if I have to date the beginning of my business career, it would have to be then.

Working entirely alone and in my spare time, production was not great – probably only about half a dozen of each line – and I think my only customers were friends. A few shops around the area were willing to buy the odd one or two, but that was the measure of my business.

It was amazing what people would buy in those zany, flower-power days. Things to hang on the wall, things in which to place your napkin, things in which to wrap your tissues – if you tried offering them to shopkeepers today they would laugh you out of the shop. My break came when the local kitchen shop in Doncaster asked me to design a tea cosy. Up till then my conception of a tea cosy was a crinoline lady knitted in pink wool, with a porcelain head, and bonnet. I must have had a rush of blood to the creative crevice in my brain, because I came up with a design which I knew was either stunning, or an unmitigated disaster. It was in the shape of a cockerel, its plumage a cascade of felt feather shapes in various tones of green, turquoise, and blue. The head had a red comb, a red dangly wattle (the bit under the chin) and a pair of beady glass eyes. My customer was thrilled and immediately ordered a dozen. I experienced for the first, but by no means the last time, that giddy feeling of panic and exhilaration which one gets on realising that demand has outstripped supply.

Instead of buying the felt in 9-square-inch pieces, I had to get the 12-inch ones, and found to my delight that you could purchase the lethal glass eyes on the ends of wires in bundles of a dozen, thus saving a penny or so. Drawing round a sixpence and cutting out the felt eyes with a pair of nail scissors was labour intensive, so when Eddie arrived home with a circular punch of the correct diameter, I really felt we were well on our way to full mechanisation. Unfortunately, they had to be punched out on the bread board, and we did splinter rather a lot of the boards, making the process somewhat counterproductive. I'm sure the circular indentations can still be found on Home Farm's stone doorstep.

Eddie was working for yet another builder's merchants in these very early days and spent a lot of time travelling the length and breadth of Northern England. This was handy because he was excited about the potential of my little cottage business, and on his travels would make impromptu visits to other kitchen shops in places as far flung as … Leeds! He would come leaping home each evening with the orders he had taken – in his lunch hour, he claims. I have recently unearthed a drawer full of our very first accounts, and they make fascinating reading.

I was still teaching at this stage, so every night I had to pick up the children from school, and ferry them around to the various activities in which children of that age *must* indulge, partly to satisfy the parents' guilt for both working, and partly to enable them to maintain credibility with their peers. Music lessons, ballet classes (not a great success where Joanna was concerned), riding, chess club, and in Jeremy's case extra maths coaching (an even bigger waste of money – he still can't divide by twelve). Home for tea – 'quality time' as it is now known – and then to bed with a couple of chapters of Enid Blyton's *The Secret Seven*, after which I would start making my cockerels.

The winter of 1970-71 was plagued by power cuts, and I spent many evenings with a candle in a jam jar, a twelve inch ruler, and scissors, frantically chopping and assembling combs, beaks and wattles. Eddie was away a great deal, so I would get up at six o'clock each morning having been in the hen run till three, rush to the municipal swimming baths, watch both offspring do fifty (well, five maybe) lengths, ram a bacon butty down them, and deliver them to their seats of learning for nine o'clock. Many a morning I had to crawl past my headmistress's office window on hands and knees, to avoid her sigh of despair at my indolence. After a year of this, I took enormous delight in handing her my resignation. I was about to be sacked anyway for flatly refusing to go on strike, something to do with dinner duties.

Eddie was, I have to say, slightly sceptical that I could make tea cosies pay as much as my teaching job, and said in desperation "Just what do you intend calling this company then?"

"Gabrielle Designs," I said without a moment's hesitation.

My parents had actually chosen 'Gay' as my middle name, but as I turned out to be such a miserable little sod, after a few weeks they changed it to Gabrielle. I shall be eternally grateful to them for that, but will never forgive them for 'Shirley'!

Once I'd announced my new status as a full-time entrepreneur, Eddie went off directly, bless him, and bought me a roll of printed satin labels to sew in my tea cosies. 'GABRIELLE DESIGNS' was printed in turquoise blue – the company colour that we used from then on.

Free from the fetters of teaching, I was deliriously happy. Home Farm was barely habitable, but I gave the spare room a coat of paint, bought a cheap sewing machine, an army surplus table, and got to work. I quickly increased my range to include an owl tea cosy and a hessian draught excluder in the form of a caterpillar. A wool fringe sewn along the bottom represented the caterpillar's feet, and brightly coloured wooden beads ran down the spine. We christened this the

'Draffakilla', which we thought was a stroke of genius, and they sold like hot cakes in a snowstorm.

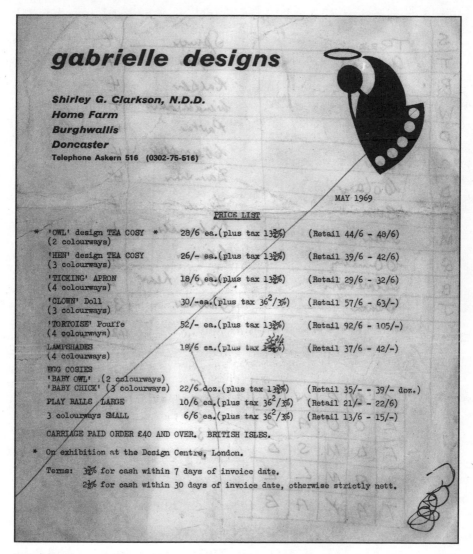

gabrielle designs

Shirley G. Clarkson, N.D.D.
Home Farm
Burghwallis
Doncaster
Telephone Askern 516   (0302-75-516)

MAY 1969

PRICE LIST

* 'OWL' design TEA COSY * (2 colourways)	28/6 ea.(plus tax 13¾%)	(Retail 44/6 - 48/6)
'HEN' design TEA COSY (3 colourways)	26/- ea.(plus tax 13¾%)	(Retail 39/6 - 42/6)
'TICKING' APRON (4 colourways)	18/6 ea.(plus tax 13¾%)	(Retail 29/6 - 32/6)
'CLOWN' Doll (3 colourways)	30/-ea.(plus tax $36^2/3$%)	(Retail 57/6 - 63/-)
'TORTOISE' Pouffe (4 colourways)	52/- ea.(plus tax 13¾%)	(Retail 92/6 - 105/-)
LAMPSHADES (4 colourways)	18/6 ea.(plus tax 13¾%)	(Retail 37/6 - 42/-)
EGG COSIES 'BABY OWL' (2 colourways) 'BABY CHICK' (3 colourways)	22/6 doz.(plus tax 13¾%)	(Retail 35/- - 39/- doz.)
PLAY BALLS LARGE	10/6 ea.(plus tax $36^2/3$%)	(Retail 21/- - 22/6)
3 colourways SMALL	6/6 ea.(plus tax $36^2/3$%)	(Retail 13/6 - 15/-)

CARRIAGE PAID ORDER £40 AND OVER.   BRITISH ISLES.

* On exhibition at the Design Centre, London.

Terms: 3¾% for cash within 7 days of invoice date.
      2½% for cash within 30 days of invoice date, otherwise strictly nett.

Conversion tables available for the "under thirty sevens".

As the range of products grew, I realised that I needed to find a new material supplier. Buying small quantities of felt at retail prices from the local haberdashery made no sense at all. My search for a new supplier led me to Bury Masco, an incredible company in Lancashire, sadly no longer in existence, which was housed in one of those glorious six-storey stone mill buildings. It employed men from up t'valley, whose world consisted of Rossendale, the chapel, and the local brass band. I was told that the reason they could make such magnificent felt was the purity of the water which flowed down from the hills. Their machinery had been purchased around the time of King Ethelred. There were no lifts in the building and the floors were connected by creaking old oak stairways made from timber salvaged from the ark, and polished by the continual dragging of lanolin-soaked bales of wool. They not only manufactured felt, but would cut it to any shape to suit customers' requirements. Clanking old machines would drop 'heads' of great tonnage onto 'pastry cutters' which would cut through forty to fifty layers of fabric. I still carry a mental picture of one worker called Walter, well into his seventies, sitting at one of these machines cutting corn plasters out of pink felt, and, incredibly, keeping count with a piece of paper and a stub of a pencil. If anyone spoke to him, he would lose count and have to tip the box out and start again.

Eddie and I went over to Lancashire (not a thing Yorkshiremen do without good reason) to see Bury Masco for the first time and were introduced to Jack Lawton, the sales manager, who in turn introduced us to Gloria, who was … just Gloria. Between them I think they held the firm together. When we explained our problem of having to buy felt at the local haberdashers, but needing maybe two yards of fifty different colours, I well remember Jack's remark – not a worldshaker, but oh so true: "Great oaks from little acorns grow." "And," he continued, "if we don't give the small people what they want they'll never get larger." With that, he proceeded to climb up and down ladders cutting off short lengths of felt for us. For some reason, the cost of that first order sticks in my memory. It was just over a hundred pounds. We drove back across the Pennines trembling at our recklessness, but you have to take these big chances in life!

Jack sadly died of cancer, but Gloria lives on. To those two individuals, I must attribute a good slice of Gabrielle Designs' success. If I could have persuaded Gloria to venture east when Bury Masco folded I would have employed her like a shot. She could sort out a problem in about two minutes, a crisis in no time at all. If I rang to say that a delivery was late, or wrong in some way or another, there would be a few blasts of "Bloody 'ell Shirley what 'ave they been doin' with your order!" and she would ring off with the immortal phrase "Leave it to me". Never in twenty years did she let me down.

They are so hazy, these early days, that it's difficult to remember exactly the order of things. I know that Eddie was using his natural sales ability to good effect. As he toured the country selling building modules (whatever they were), he would spend his lunch hour, and a few hours besides, calling on boutiques in the various towns and cities. Hen tea cosies were the No. 1 seller, and my crowning glory in 1970 was to have them displayed in the Design Centre in London. That did it, there was no stopping us!

Eddie made the decision to give up his highly paid sales job in Bristol, and join me at Gabrielle. Inevitably, that meant that cash would get even tighter until Eddie could bring in new business. We thought it only right to put the idea to the children, and having explained what it would mean in terms of hardship, Jeremy just said, "Okay, now we can we watch Thunderbirds?". A strategic meeting with the bank manager was arranged. Mr Robson had moved on, so we set up an appointment with his successor.

The meeting with the new bank manager was epic. It was fortunate that his office curtains toned beautifully with my blue hen tea cosies, and the fact that his wife was always moaning about cold tea helped. He listened sympathetically to our expansion plans, and then came the crunch question: "What about working capital?"

My housekeeping that week was £16, and Eddie had £9 in his wallet. That was it. Mr Manager graciously offered to advance us £100, which we accepted on the spot. From that day to this we never borrowed another penny from anyone.

Eddie didn't particularly enjoy telling his sales manager that he was resigning in order to sell tea cosies, but it was nothing compared to the feeling of despair we both felt when I picked him up from Sheffield Midland station driving a battered old Austin 1100, on hire. He had left his beautiful new Audi in Bristol, together with his expenses book, and this old wreck was all we could afford. We sat in the car for a moment, probably the last time we sat for twenty years, and as we watched the sun set over Park Hill flats, clutched each other and sighed, "What the hell have we done?"

That was the last moment of doubt we ever experienced.

Chapter Five – Our Acorn

My follow-up to the tea cosies was a pouffe, not a word used much in furnishing circles these days, or indeed in many other circles, but they were all the rage in the sixties. A tuffet, or a thing to sit on, gives a clearer picture. My design was in the shape of a tortoise, and made from brightly coloured felt, with patches in contrasting colours to represent the pattern of the shell, which were embroidered by machine. This was called "twirdling". It was followed by a hedgehog pouffe with a hessian back, into which strips of felt were pegged, a bit like the way our great grandmothers used strips of old shirts etc. to make fireside rugs.

Our 'Draffakilla' draught excluders sold well. Also made from hessian, they were a caterpillar shape, with a spine of coloured beads and two rows of wool fringe representing feet running along the bottom. This was before central heating had really caught on, and they were a must in every house. We also made felt balls, felt clowns, felt lampshades, and aprons with matching oven mitts. Then my pièce de résistance – a hessian hobby horse, with large black bead eyes, decorated with brightly-coloured felt flowers, a rope bridal, all mounted on a beech pole with wooden wheels on the bottom. This design too was accepted by the Design Centre. (I have a feeling standards have improved in the last twenty years. I would never have made it into the Tate Modern today.)

Eddie and I had a wonderful working relationship at that time. It wasn't always so wonderful in later years. He would leave on Monday morning to trawl a given area – it could be Scotland or Devon – and return on Friday with a bulging order book. Production and sales is always a balancing act, but our scales got seriously out of sync, with sales far outstripping production. It was a problem, but one to be enjoyed.

Keeping a lid on costs and expenses was important, and Eddie used a hard and fast rule on his sales trips: he would only spend a certain proportion of total sales any given day on his night's accommodation. If he sold nothing, he slept in the car and had a bag of chips. If the sales were reasonable, the chips came with mushy peas. If he had a good day and filled the order book, he treated himself to a decent hotel and dined in its restaurant. His lodgings varied from sharing a room with a tramp to the honeymoon suite at the Plaza.

Soon the hired car changed to a Ford Cortina, second-hand, but our own, and progressed quite rapidly upwards to an Audi, and then to a BMW. Eddie loved his cars. I couldn't give a damn what I drove, as long as it started first pull, had a heater, and I could get Jimmy Young on the radio. Jeremy obviously inherited his father's passion, but in those days it amounted to crashing thousands of Dinky cars into the skirting boards, and forcing Joanna to play hot-wheels. Poor Jo, she never stood a chance to become 'girlie'. The few dolls she had were always left out in the rain overnight, so perhaps it was never meant to be.

I recently came across a whole wedge of papers, listing Gabrielle Designs' very first accounts. Handwritten by Eddie, they show the sales to our first customers, small retailers which have almost all disappeared now to make way for the Matalans, Primarks and TK Maxxes of this world. The bestselling products were the tea cosies. Abacus, in Baker Street was our number one customer, topping the list with a dozen hen tea cosies, for which they paid £1 and 5 shillings each, making a total of £15. Also on the schedule are numerous large and small dice, which is odd because I have no memory of making these. Napkin holders and hook boards appear occasionally but didn't seem to be bestsellers, but at 5 shillings and 3 pence each, we weren't going to pay off the mortgage with those.

In amongst this bundle of documents there is a letter written by Eddie to all the miscreants who had not settled their account by the end of the week. One poor soul in Northallerton was going to be put into the hands of the receivers for an unpaid bill of £14.9.6d. If Eddie had ever followed through with this threat, I'd hate to have seen the solicitor's bill for dealing with the bandit.

I also found a very curt letter from Eddie to our accountant, complaining bitterly about the increase in his fees over the previous year. He couldn't understand why the annual charge had risen to £126.19.4d when we had improved our accounting system considerably. The poor man tried to explain that the increase in Gabrielle's turnover meant more work for him, and threw in something about inflation and wage rises. At the time, these phenomena meant nothing to me, but I'd learn quickly about them in later years.

It wasn't long before we realised that Eddie couldn't cover the entire country. If he spent a week in Scotland, what was happening to sales in the rest of Britain? So we decided to appoint some agents. The first man we took on was from Bradford, and his area was the middle chunk of England.

Very strange people, agents. Lesson One is that they are not employees, and you have virtually no control over them. A good one will work like a beaver for the first few months, establishing contacts and enthusiastically showing your goods to every shop he can find, thereby collecting his 15% commission on the first order. Then, when the repeat orders start flowing in, the agent goes to the Bahamas for a month, and the 15% keeps on rolling in. This is great for the agent but not necessarily so for the manufacturer. Also, Eddie and I liked to choose our retail customers with care, making sure our designs were right for their particular outlet and that they could sell what we sent them. It wasn't in our interests to dump a load of stock on them which they couldn't sell. Also, we wanted to be sure that customers were able to pay for the goods they ordered, because a bad debt would hit us hard. An agent doesn't have to worry so much about bad debts – all he loses is his commission – whereas the manufacturer loses the full trade value of the goods.

I can't remember how many agents we got through, but it was a lot. Eddie understood their problems because he was a salesman himself – it *is* frustrating to travel across Norfolk behind a tractor, only to find when arriving at a shop, that it's half-day closing. He once made an appointment to meet the buyer of a very large shop in Ayr, travelled the two hundred or so miles, only to be told she had a headache, and couldn't see him. He booked into a hotel for the night, and next morning was told that the buyer had gone to a funeral.

Whatever occasional problems we had with agents, the going for Gabrielle Designs was still good. In fact, sales were coming in so fast that I struggled to increase production. I had a cleaning lady called

Maureen at the time, although what she was expected to clean heaven only knows. The floors at Home Farm were mainly soil, awaiting the laying of flagstones, there was no paint on any walls, and our meagre collection of cheap furniture was stored in one room. I say cheap, but we are talking about Windsor backed chairs bought for seven and sixpence, oak kists for a pound, and best of all, a beautiful Victorian button-backed chair, bought together with a butter churn for five shillings at a farm sale.

Instead of sweeping the soil floors, I engaged Maureen's time more efficiently, by teaching her to sew heads on hens, and "twirdle" tortoise's shells. She went home each evening with plastic Asda bags full of animal parts to assemble. Her Aunty Vera was eager to help, as was her cousin Flo and pretty soon, even though we didn't realise it, we were running a cottage industry of outworkers.

Pouffes need stuffing. This was a different ball game from sewing. Off I went to my local haberdashers to enquire with what one stuffed. Kapok, that's what.

To the uninitiated, Kapok is an evil, albeit natural fibre. Its singular quality is that it is lighter than air, which would make the stuffing of pouffes well nigh impossible in space. If you let it escape, it floats imperceptibly around the house, coming to rest mainly on the butter dish. Another of its charms is that, being so light, it has to be packed into bales under immense pressure and then bound with half-inch metal bands. When the bands are cut using sharp bolt cutters, the severed ends fly in all directions, slicing anything in their path – arms, noses, scalps – anything.

For asthma sufferers like Eddie, Kapok is death, but tortoises must be stuffed, so large bags of the ghastly stuff were squeezed into the utility room, and a team of stuffers employed on an ad hoc basis to ram the tortoises to satisfactory firmness. They were then piled up in the dining room where their bottoms were stitched by Kath, the local farmer's wife.

In summer 1971, as we were leaving for our annual holiday, we thought we ought to buy a good quantity of Kapok to keep the girls going while we were away. Forgetting how incredibly light it is, I followed the salesman's advice and ordered a ton (clever fellow). It arrived two minutes after we had left for Cornwall, and the only way they were able to manoeuvre the twenty bales into the house was by removing the front door. On our return, we could only just get the door open, and found every single room of the house stacked floor to ceiling with bales.

Our staff were rather special, as the case of Dolly showed. Dolly was a very jolly soul, known (of course) as 'Jolly Dolly', aged about 30 who came to Gabrielle from Monday to Thursday, but couldn't work Fridays because of her feet. Our method of paying employees was for me to take the cash box round on Fridays, and hand out money for hours worked. Poor old Dolly. After about six weeks she asked Norma, "Do you get paid for doing this?" She enjoyed the job so much that she wasn't sure whether she should be paid for it. (As a side note, the cash box with its stack of pound notes, was an object of such fascination for Joanna that she always said that when Eddie and I died all she wanted was that box. Jeremy was no fool, and readily agreed. I really must see a solicitor and put that right before I 'go'.)

The misunderstanding with Dolly convinced us that we needed some kind of bookkeeping, so Betty, a lady in the village with some knowledge of accounting, was employed part-time. The only available space for her to work was the landing. Outside the bathroom door, we put up a card table upon which we placed Eddie's antiquated Olivetti typewriter, and she kept a very efficient set of accounts. Complicated subjects like Purchase Tax had to be mastered, and one morning, desperate to go to the lavatory, I found the Purchase Tax inspector sitting with Betty, leaning his chair against the bathroom door. I was far too in awe of him to ask him to move, and the downstairs loo was full of stuffing, so I had no choice but to jump in the car and head off to the public conveniences. I mention this to give you some idea of the sheer oddness of working at Gabrielle Designs in these years. Frankly, that never changed much.

On another of his visits, the Purchase Tax inspector found a discrepancy of 13sh 4d in our ledgers, and then accidentally dropped a ring binder on the floor, breaking it. On the cover of the binder was stuck a price ticket for 13sh 6d, so – no kidding – Eddie made him give us two pence, to make things all square. You can't win the war against bureaucrats, but occasionally Fate grants you little victories over them, and very pleasurable they are too.

Throughout 1971 sales continued to grow, and it soon became clear who the production bottleneck was: me! Designing, sourcing fabric, cutting and stitching were gumming up the production line. Vera could twirdle faster than I could cut, so help was needed in the spare room. After a disastrous engagement of Lying Lillian who could just as well have been called Thieving Lillian, we rang my old stamping ground, Doncaster School of Art. They recommended a young girl of Polish parenthood called Kristina who had just completed a design course there. She was nineteen, and stayed with us almost continuously until she was forty-four. She was so shy and retiring, and arrived the first morning, late, having missed the bus, the only bus, clutching a tin of rice pudding for her lunch. Kristina had phenomenal talent, and if she had only had more confidence would have made a name for herself in the design world. She was a brilliant calligrapher, dress designer, and seamstress, she could cook, and was a wonderful babysitter. She played an important part in Gabrielle Designs, which I will come to soon.

Our life was totally absorbed with the business, but we had to continue our efforts to make Home Farm habitable, or at least hygienic enough to prevent the local council from taking the children into care. Yorkshire flagstones were laid on all the ground floors, which made it easier to sweep up the Kapok. We had a 9-inch black and white television somewhere, but never had time to switch it on. Plugged into it was what I suppose must have been the very first Game Boy, an electronic display of a tennis court, with a ball which moved from one side of the screen to the other. I think it was called Pong, or possibly Ping. The two players each had a remote 'bat', which you used to hit the ball and project it back across the net. I wish we'd kept this game. It was far better than some of the modern violent blockbusters on which my grandchildren spend so much time.

Our tiny hamlet of Burghwallis was very isolated, with no pub, school, or shop, and as there was only one bus per day, the children had to be continually ferried hither and thither to friends' houses for parties etc. The bus usually arrived on time, but there was a day when one of our Springer Spaniels, called 'Numbers' was reported to be fornicating on the village war memorial, and the bus wasn't able to pass. She was called Numbers because she was the last to be born to her mother 'Thing' (Jeremy's choice of name), and her siblings were Genesis, Exodus, Leviticus, Deuteronomy, and Joshua. If there had been any more we would have had to rush for the Bible.

At Home Farm the children had the luxury of a bedroom each, but Eddie and I had to share ours with hundreds of flatpack cardboard boxes, our bedroom being the only storage space left in the house. During one of Eddie's many bouts of bronchitis, I had to summon the local GP who arrived whilst I was coping with a major crisis – the hedgehogs' prickles were falling out. I didn't have time to escort him to Eddie's room, so just gesticulated in the general direction. A few minutes later he reappeared and said that he couldn't find Eddie. All he could hear was a desperate wheezing coming from behind a pile of cartons! Poor Eddie, he always maintained that his mother had made his asthma worse by continually fussing over him, but this was going from the sublime to the ridiculous.

At vast expense, we installed central heating in Home Farm, but we couldn't run the boiler in the day as it made the Kapok circulate too much, which was bad for Eddie's asthma. I would love to know what today's health and safety czars would think of our working conditions back then. I expect we'd be slapped with enforcement notices and closed down within an hour.

Our employee relations were also rather unorthodox. For instance, one of the tasks in the tea cosy production line was to glue together their foam linings. For this, we relied on Betty's son who used to bring his girlfriend round in the evenings, and they would earn a little pin money by squeezing large bottles of Copydex around. I was slightly alarmed by their behaviour, which wasn't confined to the task at hand, but at least the girlfriend didn't become pregnant like our babysitter. Her joining the club was no great shock because we had found a trouser button on the hearth rug the next morning.

Over time, the kitchen of Home Farm was transformed and became a stunning room. We had tested the bank manager's patience to the limit by laying the most expensive, lovely Welsh Rowaban tiles. They were a beautiful shade of terracotta, and with the dark oak beams and scrubbed pine table, it is a room I will always remember with affection. We had a large kitchen table running the length of the room, and at my position at one end was the cutlery drawer. I became so fed up with people continually asking for a teaspoon, that I tied one from the beam above each chair on a length of elastic. Not one visitor to the house ever asked why we had spoons dangling from the beams. Each day, the staff and I sat down around this table and devoured our sarnics, or, if Eddie was not on his travels, he would make us homemade soup and rice pudding. Pancakes were a favourite with everyone (but not if I'd made them).

The tortoises, hedgehogs, owls and hens were packed each morning, and collected each afternoon by the carrier, BRS, as it was in those days. A delightful character named Arthur used to manoeuvre his wagon into the yard, and if we hadn't quite finished the packing, he would sit and join us for a bowl of something hot. Thirty years later, I still found carrier drivers amongst the most amiable, patient and tolerant, of men. Unfortunately, one of our early setbacks was in Christmas 1970 when BRS went on strike, which meant all our boxes were holed up in some warehouse going nowhere. These were crucial Christmas orders, so to avoid letting down our customers we had to duplicate all consignments, and send them by Royal Mail. Still, it didn't put me off Arthur, and he continued to enjoy our soup.

Surrounding the main farmhouse was a cluster of pigsties, cowsheds, and barns, all connected by a fold yard, in which was housed a wonderful collection of cattle. They would lumber up to the kitchen window, and low with great belly moos. We grew to love them, and gave them names after people we knew. The timid weedy one was named Hamilton, after Jeremy's prep school headmaster. The other bullies always pushed him out of the feeding trough, and how we rejoiced when, as his mates were carted off to the cattle market, little Hamilton was left behind to enjoy another season of fattening.

The next year Hamilton had to find a new home, because Gabrielle Designs needed his yard. The canny old farmer, realising it was a seller's market, upped the price of each barn as it was required by us, with the result that we paid twice as much for a roofless shed as we had for the house itself. We converted each barn as it became available into design and cutting rooms, sewing rooms, and an office for Betty.

Neither Eddie nor I had any formal business training. As Gabrielle Designs grew, we just used our common sense to adapt. If we needed more equipment, we bought it. If we needed more staff, we employed them. Everything was decided on the hoof. There was no business plan to follow, no shareholders to whom we had to explain our 'corporate strategy'. Thank goodness for that, because I don't know what it means.

In the seventies there was an organisation called CoSIRA – the Council for Small Industries in Rural Areas. We were introduced to them, and in some respects they were invaluable. Bearded worthies in cords and large brogues would give advice on accountancy, marketing, personnel – all manner of things – to help stupid entrepreneurs run their business. I think we posed something of a challenge to CoSIRA. They were fascinated by our unorthodox methods.

As part of the service, we were sent a 'Time-and-Motion' man to help speed up production. I have never giggled so much since my school days when someone farted in chapel. Looking back it was shameful of me, but he was such an earnest young man, with his clipboard and the sense of humour of a lobster. He spent time observing each of our 'departments' over a period of three days, and took copious notes of our methods. Surprised at the lack of any clock in the office, he asked Betty:

"How do you know when it's time to go home?"

"Oh," she replied, "I usually leave when the sun goes behind the chimney pot."

"And what if it's a cloudy day?"

"Well, I just work overtime."

Kristina came under scrutiny as she cut strips of felt to make hedgehog prickles. When our friend asked how she knew how long to make each strip she explained that it was two little things on the ruler past the crack in the table.

He was a completely flummoxed by our stock sheets, especially when two hundred black beads used for hedgehog's noses disappeared from the list, only to reappear again as horse's eyeballs. He just couldn't understand that a bead, or a piece of felt, or a length of braid, could be used in all sorts of different ways at Gabrielle. It could be a body part for a hen tea cosy or a Draffakilla or a pouffe.

 "How do you know when you are getting short of purple cotton?" he once asked me. I explained that I took the lid off the box and said, "Good gracious me, we are running out of purple cotton".

That was far too simple for him. He insisted on showing me how to plot a graph of our stock position.

"It will tell you when you are getting low on a certain component," he promised.

The way I saw it, if I could remember to fill in the graph I might as well spend that time actually ordering the cotton. Call me a stuck-in-the-mud, but till the day I retired from Gabrielle, I stuck with my old-fashioned 'system'.

Mind you, stocktaking was a nightmare. I remember once asking one of the girls to count how many giraffe eyes we had. These came complete with lids and long lashes, on cards of one hundred. When I found her hours later at about two thousand, one hundred and sixty four, I asked why she hadn't realised there were ten rows of ten eyes on each card, making one hundred per card, and all she had to do was count up the number of cards in stock and multiply that by one hundred. She looked puzzled.

"What do you mean by multiply?" she said, brow furrowed.

"Well," I said, "you count the eyes across, and then times it by the number down".

"Oh, you mean *timesing*. We did *timesing*!"

The stuffing room was another challenge, a law unto itself really. Brave was the person who dared to criticise its methods. The girls in there used wonderful gadgets which we called 'plonkers'! They were smooth sticks with a pear-shaped handle fixed on the end, and were used to ram the stuffing tightly into the item being stuffed. Watching the girls stuffing away with their plonkers, Mr Time-and-Motion asked Cheryl, "Have you always been a plonker?" to which he received the well-deserved reply, "No I chuffing 'aven't!"

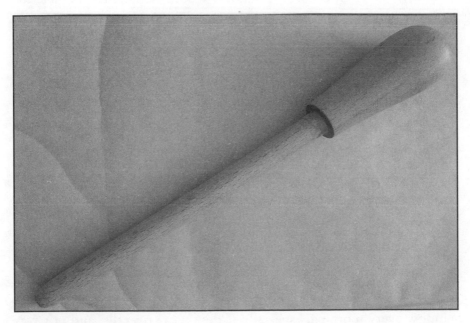

A real plonker.

When he finally sent through his report, he suggested that we made our plonkers curved to make it easier to plonk round corners. The diagram which accompanied this suggestion was not fit to be sent through the mail, and provoked unprintable comments amongst our band of happy stuffers.

Another practice which was deemed inefficient was our method of delivering work to the outworkers. This job was the responsibility of Mrs Moses. Typically, she would take out my recently-purchased green Volkswagen Beetle first thing on Friday morning to do the deliveries, then later in the morning, she would go on a second trip to fetch the fish and chips for lunch, it being Friday. I seem to remember on one of her trips she turned my beautiful new VW Beetle over, doing a considerable amount of damage. We were away for the night and Betty, the ever-devoted secretary, rang the garage to ask if it could be mended by the morning, and then Mr and Mrs Clarkson will never know.

Our friend from CoSIRA thought it would be more economical for Mrs Moses to deliver the work on the same journey as the one to the chip shop. What he didn't realise was that one of our outworkers, Mrs Hayes, left for her hospital appointment at eleven, and the work couldn't be delivered after that, or her dog would eat it. They don't teach that sort of thing in civil service manuals.

The well-meaning but often barmy recommendations of CoSIRA were easily dealt with compared to the attention we received from another quarter – our immediate neighbour. Although we were running, to our minds, a quiet little cottage business, our neighbour disagreed. She was a difficult lady at the best of times, and a degree of jealousy couldn't be ruled out. For whatever reason, she took exception to the half dozen or so girls alighting from the bus and cycling past her window every morning, especially if they wore overalls, and nor was she keen on the two or three delivery vans which reversed down the lane every day. The children were told that when they cycled past her window, they must keep pedalling, because if they free-wheeled it caused an irritating ticking noise. I have to admit that on hot sunny afternoons, when the stuffers were sitting in the garden doing their plonking, there was a certain amount of hilarity and a little community singing of the latest pop hit, but it was a real shock when the chairman of the parish council knocked on our door and invited Eddie and me to attend the village hall that evening. Parish council meetings are not high on my list of exciting things to do in life, so I politely declined, but on being told it was a protest meeting convened by our neighbour to have Gabrielle Designs closed down, I thought again. Eddie was travelling in Scotland that day and had to make the journey south in double-quick time to get to the meeting.

The hall was packed. Mrs H. rose and read a long list of vehicle registration numbers that she had noted passing her window in recent days/weeks/months. She must have spent her entire day twitching curtains. I recognised one or two of the registrations – my father's Rover, the coal merchant, the oil delivery tanker, a farm tractor, and an assortment of friends who had called in for a drink. She then produced a branch of a Laburnum tree which she alleged had been broken off by the BRS lorry. The older I become, the more I realise what is meant by a "back yarder", as our solicitor called it. Very sad affairs, and types I have struggled to avoid ever since.

The Stuffing Gang.

To my mind, nearly all neighbourly disputes can be solved with a friendly call, tact, and a bottle of something to share. We tried this with Mrs H., but she refused to come out of the kitchen, choosing instead to hurl insults at us through the hatchway.

The Parish Council saw reason and took no further action against us, so we continued in business, though always in a sweat that a delivery lorry might accidentally catch her Laburnum on its way up or down the lane.

Chapter Six – Our Sapling

For Christmas each year, I made a soft toy to sit on the top of the children's stockings. One year I made a complete set of Winnie the Pooh characters – Pooh in mustard towelling, Eeyore in grey felt, and Tigger with black stripes painted on to his yellow hessian body. Jeremy and Joanna both treasured these one-offs and they became a kind of family tradition. In the attic to this day I have some moth-eared creatures with one eye, torn-off limbs and appendectomy scars.

1971s choice of toy changed all our lives dramatically, and with such swiftness that we hardly realised what was happening. A friend recommended that I buy a book for the children entitled *A Bear Called Paddington*, by Michael Bond. It was all about a delightful little bear called Paddington, and was illustrated by Peggy Fortnum. The illustrations were only simple pen and ink sketches, but the movements and character that this lady managed to convey were charming. Jeremy and Joanna loved the stories. They contained everything a child wants in a book: a bear, marmalade, sticky buns, ice cream, glue, soap suds, together with a character that epitomised what every adult admires:

innocence, vulnerability, kindness, humour, politeness, and an unshakeable love and loyalty towards his friends.

Michael Bond, with Paddington in pride of place.

My problem of what to make for the children's stocking in 1971 was solved when I read Michael's book. I bought a couple of yards of fur fabric from Doncaster market, and with bits of felt leftover from the tea cosies, together with some glass eyes and plastic noses, set about designing the bear. I was too busy to spend much time on the toys, so after studying Peggy Fortnum's drawings, I left Kristina to do the initial cutting and stitching whilst I rushed off on my usual afternoon school run, ferrying, comforting, smacking (you were allowed to in those days), screaming, and doing all the things that frustrated mothers do in traffic jams.

When I finally got home, and had served up the chips and sausages etc., it was past the hour when the sun vanished behind the chimney pot, and the staff, including Kristina, had all gone home, which was unusual for her as she often stayed well into the evening and joined Eddie and me for the nightly gin or vodka, before heading home in my Audi.

I went across the yard to the workrooms, and there, sitting on the table was the little fellow who was ultimately to change our lives. Unmistakably Paddington! He had a navy blue duffle coat and a light blue hat, if my memory serves me right. Kristina had added a little touch of her own by giving him a posy of flowers in his hand, and a little pair of rimless spectacles perched on the end of his nose. I stood and gazed at him for a long time, and distinctly remember thinking, "He's got it".

I recognised something in Paddington that was special, and knew immediately that this design wasn't just going to sit atop Jeremy and Joanna's Christmas stocking; it was going to become a Gabrielle product.

Much later, when Michael Bond wrote his autobiography, he recalled his reaction on first seeing our Paddington Bear:

Originally made one Christmas as a present for Shirley's and her husband Eddie's children Jeremy and Joanna it [the stuffed bear] remains a classic of its kind – one which still gives me pleasure whenever I see it – and it served as a kind of yardstick when judging other products. Some things, like Concorde and the Jaguar XK 120, look right from the word go. It was created with love and it was born with that indefinable something known as star quality. You either have it or you don't.

That passage makes me feel just a little proud whenever I read it. I'm very grateful to Michael, and equally thankful to Kristina for her help in that first creation.

When Eddie returned home from his travels that evening, my father, who over the last few years had adopted the title of "Bumper", being the nearest to "Grandpa" that Jeremy could manage, had arrived for his customary weekly supper. A lovable GP of the old school, he maintained that all a doctor needed most of the time was a box of tissues on his desk, and time to listen. He was very perceptive and wise. I valued his opinions on everything, as everyone did, and they usually proved to be right.

The three of us sat and gazed at 'Bear' sitting in an armchair staring across the room at us, and we all agreed he had the look of greatness about to descend upon him. You notice I refer to him as 'Bear' because at that time our ignorance of things financial was matched only by our ignorance of things legal. We were vaguely aware of something called copyright, but what it entailed was a mystery to us, so we thought it best to play safe, and not call 'Bear', 'Paddington'. I have to say, in the early seventies relatively few people had ever heard of Paddington. The books had been successful for some time, but of course only a fraction of the population are readers.

Jeremy and Joanna received their Christmas toy, and were delighted. When they showed Bear to their friends there were more squeals of delight, and when the parents of those friends arrived to pick up their children, the squeals would turn to demands: "I want a Paddington like Joanna!" Everyone who saw Bear and who knew Michael Bond's books made the connection between the two and – better than that – loved what we had done. It was that reaction, above all, that convinced us that we should turn Bear into a commercial product.

We obviously had to market him, but, as mentioned, we didn't think we could call him Paddington, so we hit on a brilliant idea: we would sell him as 'The Earl of Burghwallis'. That way no one could accuse us of breaching copyright! It's amazing that two adults could be so naïve, but we were.

Off went Eddie to London, with a Bear to show potential customers. His first call was the lovely shop, sadly now gone – as have so many of our first customers – called Abacus, situated on the corner of Baker Street and George Street. They had already been great buyers of the tea cosies. As Eddie walked in with Bear, cries of "It's Paddington!" echoed round the shop from customers and staff alike. Obviously, a very literate class of shopper around Baker Street.

"No, no!" cried Eddie, "this is the Earl of Burghwallis!", which did little to satisfy the proprietor, who maintained it was the nearest thing to a real Paddington that he had ever seen.

Flushed with this success, and with the order in his pocket book, Eddie marched off to Hamleys and a few other small boutiques in the area with whom he had good trade relations. It was like taking candy from a baby. Every shop loved Bear and placed an order on the spot. After noting the order, Eddie told the customer that under no circumstances were they to call him Paddington. We still didn't really know why, but were very quickly to learn.

This dramatic upsurge of business created wonderful problems back in the old homestead. I seem to remember we doubled the workforce, now totalling about ten, we invested in an industrial sewing machine, hitherto having managed with my old domestic Pfaff. More plonkers were commissioned from Norma's husband, a builder, and Kapok stuffing had to be bought in even bigger bulk.

Just when all the wheels of big business had been set in motion, the first of probably a few thousand blows beset us. I was alone in the office one April morning in 1972, and took a telephone call from a very polite gentleman who enquired if we made the wonderful Paddington Bears he had heard about. Flattered by his praise, and suspecting nothing, I replied that indeed we did. He then asked where he could buy one in London, as his wife was a keen reader of the Paddington books and he wanted to give her a bear as a present. Without a moment's hesitation I advised him to try Hamleys as I knew they had stock. As I replaced the receiver after my call something told me I had just made a terrible mistake.

By coincidence Eddie was in London that morning. Heading down Baker Street he saw to his horror a large banner slung across the road, with letters a foot high, announcing, "Paddington Bear comes to town". That was it. Game over!

Sure enough the following morning an official looking envelope arrived with a daunting red frank stamp on the front saying 'Crawley & de Reya, Solicitors'.

We didn't keep that letter, I wish we had, but in essence it said, "Give ovver", which every Yorkshireman would understand. Translated into legal speak it read approximately as follows:

 It has come to our notice blah blah ... infringement of copyright blah blah ... and we the undersigned ... insist that you cease forthwith ... substantial damages ... etc.

I seem to remember the dreaded word copyright was liberally scattered here and there. I felt a bit peeved, but wasn't at all surprised. We knew we were doing something wrong but thought there was an odds-on chance we would get away with it. It was a real bugger. Just as things were beginning to look really good ...

Eddie and I read the letter a few times over the kitchen table and discussed what to do. We decided to take the bull by the horns, ring the solicitor's office, speak to the signatory, Mr Edlmann, and see if we could salvage something from the situation. I never met the gentleman sadly, but Eddie always said that that's exactly what he was, a gentleman. He suggested a meeting with Mr Bond at his firm's offices in Piccadilly and invited Eddie to bring a bear along. Eddie was not over confident, but off he went on 2nd May, clutching a newly-minted PB under his arm, and as he entered the lift, he found himself standing beside a white-haired, very distinguished looking man, who said, "You must be Mr Clarkson". Yes, it was Michael.

From that first meeting in an unexceptional office lift, a rapport was established between the two men which was very special. After Eddie died Michael's feelings were made clear, again in his autobiography. He reflects in the last chapter on all the people he has admired in his life. He loves to sit outside the Café de la Paix in Paris, where legend has it that if you sit long enough, someone you know will pass by. He writes:

Eddie Clarkson will never pass by [no, he would have dragged you in and bought you a drink] and that is sad, because in his life he was the most convivial of companions, full of unstinting Yorkshire hospitality, yet stubborn as a mule. He was always the best of friends, and Paddington and I have lost a great champion.

I couldn't agree more, Michael.

But all that was much later. In Mr Edlmann's offices on May 2nd, Eddie and Michael had a potentially difficult situation to resolve. Michael opened the proceedings by saying that he wanted to make it quite clear that he had no intention of stopping us making Paddington; it was indeed the finest bear he had ever seen, he loved the whole concept, and there was only one thing to discuss – royalties. Although everyone nowadays understands what royalties are, in those days the whole subject was in its infancy. The idea of making soft toys under licence to an author was very new, but Mr Edlmann obviously had a shrewd legal mind and was far-sighted enough to see the potential of Paddington Bear as a brand. Fortunately, he was also a reasonable man.

MICHAEL BOND

██████████
████████
HASLEMERE,
SURREY.
TEL ██████

10th May, 1972.

Mr. E.G.Clarkson,
Gabrielle Designs,
Home Farm,
Burghwallis,
Doncaster,
Yorkshire.

Dear Mr. Clarkson,

Many thanks for your letter of May 3rd; also for Paddington,
who arrived safe and sound on Saturday last - complete with
the proceeds of the 'whip round'.

He really is a super bear, with lots of character. My daughter
removed his duffle coat and boots last night (something I must
admit I hadn't done) and we were most impressed.

I hope we can come to an agreement as I'm sure it will be
to both our benefit, and if this proves possible there are
a number of avenues other than your normal outlets that I
think could well be explored. I would, for instance, like
to show one to Collins, who may be interested in buying a
number for promotion purposes. Also, I think it might be as
well to incorporate your cheque in the wording of any such
agreement in order to tie up the loose ends.

It was nice meeting you the other day and I hope we shall
be able to meet again in the not too distant future. As it
happens I shall be travelling North on Monday next (May 15th)
and could make a detour to Burghwallis, but if this is at
all inconvenient perhaps you could let me know.

Yours sincerely,

Michael Bond

An agreement was reached with which both sides were happy. I
never really understood how the percentages and sliding scales worked
– I had far more important things to worry about, what with plonking
and stuffing – so I left the negotiations to Eddie and Nicholas

Durbridge, who handled Michael's commercial affairs. In essence, Gabrielle Designs was granted the exclusive right to sell Paddington Bears worldwide, and was guaranteed legal protection against any impostor who dared to make any graven images. Up to that moment the word 'pirate' conjured up in my mind wild men from Penzance with daggers in their teeth and skull and crossbones on their hats. I was to discover later what their modern day counterparts are, and how damaging they can be to a business.

It was not till many years later that we learned *how* Michael Bond had discovered that we were making his bears. Eddie had sold some to a lovely little boutique in Haslemere, Surrey, where Michael and his wife at that time, Brenda, were living. The owner of the shop knew Michael quite well, so not unnaturally rang him up to congratulate him on this wonderful line of bears that he had come across. Nicholas was detailed to look into the matter!

Before the licence agreement was signed Michael must have had some last-minute doubts about whether we were the right people to make Paddington. I don't think any of us at that stage realised that this furry little character would become an international star selling in hundreds of thousands, but Michael wanted to be sure that we were up to the job. Always the diplomat, he didn't actually say, "I'm coming up to Yorkshire to suss you out, because you look a bit dozy to me". Instead, he made an excuse that he had to come to Wetherby to visit the library there, and thought it might be a good idea to pop in and "see the factory".

Amongst Eddie's many talents he was a fantastic cook, and as we soon learned, Michael was a gourmet. We pushed the boat out for his visit, and prepared some very special Scotch salmon, Jersey Royal potatoes, and green salad, all washed down with a rather nice Chablis.

Whether it was this that captivated Michael, or the rugged simplicity of our local "stuffers", sitting in the summer sunshine ramming their plonkers hither and thither, I don't know, but he apparently wrote a letter to his agent afterwards, saying what a delightful setting it was in which to have his beloved bears created. He described Home Farm as a factory cunningly disguised as a village. The literary agent was a wonderful gentleman by the name of Harvey Unna, a German Jew, formerly an eminent judge in Germany, who had fled to England in the early thirties. He had gold-rimmed half spectacles perched on the end of his nose, and a twinkle in his eye, although it was difficult to discern the twinkle during some of the battles we had over the years. I'd hate to have come up before him charged with murder in his judging days.

Anyway, the important thing was that Michael was captivated by our ramshackle set-up. If he hadn't have been, Gabrielle Designs' foray into Paddington Bears would have been short-lived.

We registered our official Paddington Bear design on May 1st 1972, but just before we finally made him legitimate, Eddie and I made an ill-conceived and ill-fated trip to Cologne. We had been advised by the Board of Trade at that time of a 'Housewares Fair' taking place in March. "That's where we need to be," said Eddie "that's going to get us into exporting in a big way." God! I can't believe how green and stupid we were.

We booked the stand in conjunction with other companies from the UK, filled the car with samples, and with nothing more than our passports, set off. Docking in Ostend at around 5 o'clock on Friday evening, we approached customs with a cheery smile. They were more than a little concerned about the contents of the car, hobby-horse heads poking out of the rear windows, Draffakillas along the parcel shelf. We explained that we were on our way to a trade fair. Silly move!

Apparently you need 'green forms' for this – odd how the colour sticks in my mind, thirty years on. I can't remember what they were for, but we certainly hadn't got any. To obtain said forms required a visit to some office which closed at 4.30pm on Fridays and didn't reopen until Monday morning. Our fair opened on Saturday.

Now, say what you like about the Belgians, but there is, or was, a customs officer at Ostend in 1972 with a heart the size of a bucket. Seeing my tear-stained face, he took Eddie to one side, and told him to keep the engine running, wait until the man on the gate went into the cabin for his cocoa, and then make a dash for it. I now know what it feels like to be James Bond. That Audi made nought to sixty in less than a second, in a haze of blue smoke, and we belted off to Cologne not realising that we had to cross two more border controls on the way. I can't remember what happened at the Dutch and German borders, but we must have made it or we would still be there.

As we set up our stand, it became perfectly obvious that the whole thing would be a waste of time for us. Looking around at neighbouring exhibitors we saw nothing but pots, pans, kettles, cutlery, wash tubs, and buckets. Housewares means housewares, not toys and humpty-dumpty pouffettes. The final embarrassment was putting 'Paddington' out on the floor in front of the stand. Imagine a German department store buyer on a mission to buy the latest design in cheese graters seeing this little furry creature on the stand next door. I have to say, they were fascinated. "Vot exactly does he do, does he valk, talk, or beat a drum? Nein! Vell vot use is he?" So typical of the Germans – anything without a practical purpose is considered to be a waste of money. I remember receiving a letter from an angry lady many years later: "I've paid £25 for this bear and he doesn't do anything." I don't quite know what she wanted him to do. We sold not one mark's worth of anything in

Cologne, but were wined and dined every night by a wonderful British army officer and his wife stationed nearby.

Nothing could dampen our spirits. As we crossed the Channel with a car just as full as when we set out, we were buoyed by the knowledge that the shops at home had instantly loved Paddington Bear and that, thanks to Michael Bond, our little business was now the exclusive worldwide manufacturer.

At the tender age of five in 1939.

Eddie and me on our wedding day, what a perm!

Pat and me at the Rotary Ball, in that pink dress, note the hanky.

My original owl and hen tea cosies.

The hedgehog and tortoise pouffes.

The "Draffakilla" draught excluder.

A selection of original, handmade Gabrielle Designs products, circa 1971.

Joan, June, Kristina & Irene, the 4 stalwarts.

Me at my trusty sewing machine, circa 1973.

"Plonking" Paddingtons at Home Farm, circa 1973.

Eddie and me outside Home Farm,
Burghwallis.

Home Farm cowsheds, 1963.

. . . after conversion into office and workrooms, 1970.

In or out of bed~ Still the smartest bear

gabrielle designs

The Bear Garden, Great North Road, Adwick-Le Street, Doncaster
Telephone: Doncaster

Presenting our first 'Sit~Down' PADDINGTON BEAR (wearing paw~mark wellies)

gabrielle designs

GABRIELLE DESIGNS LIMITED
The Bear Garden, Great North Road,
Adwick Le Street, Doncaster,
South Yorkshire DN6 7BB
Telephone: Doncaster (0302) 721282

Paddington Bear in touch with the world

Paddington Bear's new dressing gown

gabrielle designs

Home Farm, Burghwallis,
Doncaster, Yorkshire, DN6 9JN.
Telephone: Doncaster 700516 (0302 700516)

abrielle designs

rielle Designs Ltd. Home Farm Burghwallis
ncaster, Yorkshire, England. Tel.(0302)700516

And now: For all those who think that good things come in little parcels... A pint~size Paddington!

Clothing subject to
Copyright (C) 1978
Gabrielle Designs
Design Reg. No. 9
Applied for Worl

gabrielle designs

Gabrielle Designs Limited
Home Farm Burghwallis, Doncaster
Yorkshire. Tel. (0302) 700516

This Bear protected by copyright (C) and design registration world

A selection of promotional flyers showing the different Paddingtons.

Happy times on Sizzler with Eddie, Joanna and Jillie.

The Bear Garden.

Meanwhile in the machine room at The Bear Garden, 1980.

Me and Graham at a trade fair in the early eighties.

Eddie and me with Keith, Jim and Captain Beaky and His Band.

Some of the other products created by Gabrielle Designs.

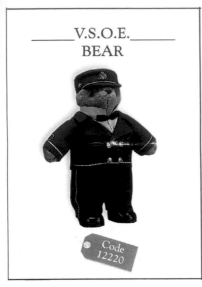

V.S.O.E.
BEAR

Code
12220

The Venice Simplon-Orient-Express
'Steward' bear.

Stephen (on the right) celebrating the sale of Gabrielle
Designs.

The 'Henry' bear, early
1980s.

Jeremy and Jo at a fair with
Welephant. (Jo's is the orange juice.)

Paddington and me, 30
years on, still firm friends.

Chapter Seven – Our Oak Tree

1973 went by in a blur of excitement, frustration, panic, but most of all, unbelievable happiness. We had acquired world rights on Paddington, and Eddie was in a salesman's paradise, selling a product that every buyer in every shop, boutique, and department store in the world was clamouring for. We were at that time the only licensor of Paddington, and had all the backing we could ever need from Michael and Harvey, who were as excited about our success as we were. I have a letter from Michael in August of our first year congratulating us on our sales. At that point, we had sold about 1,800 bears. Little did we imagine how steeply the sales graph would climb from then on.

The initial selling was done by Eddie, tearing around the country visiting shops and stores, but once people saw Paddington, he simply sold by word of mouth. We never needed to advertise in trade magazines, nor did we attend fairs in the early days. We were far too busy coping with the phenomenal pile of orders. So many people have suggested reasons for this, and they all come to basically the same conclusion: it was the character of Paddington himself – that helpless appeal of the little bear lost, who was just begging to be picked up, and loved.

To cope with demand, the workrooms at Home Farm were running flat out, and resembled an explosion in a mattress factory. Such was our arrogance that when Harrods rang to place their first order, Eddie cheekily asked them for their address. When the buyer said "Knightsbridge", he couldn't resist saying "What number?"

Although our bear design had been modelled on what we read and saw in Michael's books, it concerned me that they wouldn't stand up, so we bought some children's Wellington boots, size four, from the local shoe shop. In the books Paddington didn't wear Wellingtons when he arrived from Peru, but we all agreed he looked much better standing up, so a chapter was written in Michael's next book explaining how this resourceful little bear had acquired his Wellingtons.

According to the story, he had gone to Barkridges Store in London (no prizes for guessing which shop this represented) and whilst there had had an exciting adventure, all to do with pyjamas which were not selling very well, due to the fact that they were hideous. Paddington ended up wearing a pair in Barkridges shop window, and the sales rocketed, every last pair being sold. As a reward the manager let him choose whatever took his eye. He chose a pair of shiny red Wellingtons.

This neat little tale solved the conundrum of why Paddington wore Wellingtons, and was constructed entirely to justify us putting our bear in wellies.

The problem then bounced back on us because we had to find a supplier who could make bulk quantities of PB-sized Wellingtons. We certainly couldn't carry on buying them from our local shoe shop so we approached Dunlop who were delighted at the idea of flogging all their size four 'seconds' to us. The trouble was, they couldn't make enough seconds to satisfy our demand, so we started taking their size fives as well. Then we had to buy their 'perfects' as well as their seconds, and of course they were more expensive. That lasted for about a month, until a listener on Radio 2's Jimmy Young show rang in to complain that it was impossible to find size four or five boots for her toddlers. Mr Young had done his research, and announced that it was all Paddington Bear's fault. We had, he said, mopped up all the available boots. Even today I have great difficulty in feigning amazement when the umpteenth friend relates a story of how their little grandchild had come to visit on a wet day, and had forgotten his wellies, "You'll never guess what we did?" One runs out of different ways of expressing incredulity.

Part of the problem for Dunlop was that their manufacturing process was designed in such a way that if they made a pair of size 4 boots they also had to make a pair of size 5s, 6s, 7s, 8s and 9s. This meant that if they fulfilled our orders for the smaller sizes, they were left with excess stock of the larger ones, so all our extra business was a two-edged sword for them. Eventually Dunlop had to admit defeat and we were faced with the daunting task of finding an alternative manufacturer. Ringing large shoe manufacturers around Northamptonshire and asking if they could make Wellingtons for bears elicited some strange replies – one man told me he had made shoes for sheep during a foot and mouth crisis, but bears were something else.

It was while I was on my hunt for boots that I met one of the most charismatic men I have ever had the privilege of knowing: Mr Ormerod, who owned The Lancashire Sock Company in Rawtenstall. A lovely man, with a twinkle in his eyes, he always wore a collarless 'grandad' shirt and a brown overall, with a blue biro sticking out of the breast pocket. His business made our felt supplier, Bury Masco, look like ICI. Its main product was odour eaters, inner soles that help to absorb sweat, but in the far corner of its antiquated mill there was a machine capable of making plastic boots. It was a large circular carousel-type contraption with eight stations housing moulds – four for the uppers and four for the soles. This enabled us to design a sole plate, which had 'P.B.' and a paw mark on it.

As the machine slowly rotated, liquid PVC was poured into the machine from a bucket high up on a gantry. The whole operation was controlled by Fred. He was responsible for pulling each boot from the mould, at the same time running up a ladder, and mixing different coloured dyes with the PVC. He had a number of unexplained plasters on his face, and scorch marks on his hands, caused by pulling the boots from the machine whilst still hot.

The finished boots were lined up on a shelf, and one couldn't help noticing that there was a certain colour variation in them, especially the blue ones. "Ah," said Mr Ormerod, "that's when Fred goes for a pee." I was never sure whether he meant that Fred actually pee-ed in the dye buckets, or just that his time away from the machine caused the PVC colour to change. I like to think the first.

We had a wonderful working relationship with The Lancashire Sock Company for many years. The company is still manufacturing odour eaters, ironing board covers and synthetic chamois leathers, and is now managed by Mr Ormerod's son.

It was very difficult finding a substitute for The Lancashire Sock Company. I seem to remember making illicit trips to Accrington every Saturday morning to collect boxfulls of boots from the back door of a lock-up. I can't remember why, but I think they were trading illegally. Eventually we found an established manufacturer in Northampton, who were fine, but they never provided the laughs we had in Rawtenstall.

gabrielle designs

Shirley G. Clarkson, N.D.D.
Home Farm
Burghwallis
Doncaster
Yorkshire, DN6 9JN, England
Telephone Askern 516 ▮▮▮▮

26th May 1972.

Dear

PADDINGTON BEAR

The ever increasing success of our new design was never anticipated and what
we hoped would never happen has happened.   Such is the demand for Paddington
that there is now an imbalance in our production with our other designs.
Paddington was put on to the market at a much lower profit margin than our
other designs as we anticipated only a reasonable response.   It is now
abundantly clear that he must make his own contribution.

In addition to this, since costing Paddington when Dunlop's assured us that
they could suffice our needs with seconds quality wellington boots, they have
now informed us that we have exhausted their supplies and must now buy first
quality boots at considerable extra cost.   Paddington says this is very right
and proper!   We must therefore very reluctantly increase the cost to take
effect immediately to £4.20, retail price range now £7.875 to £8.40.   Orders
we have on hand will be honoured at the old price and we give an assurance
that these new prices are now firm until 1973.

Yours sincerely,
GABRIELLE DESIGNS.

Edward G. Clarkson.

Victims of our own success: A letter to our customers about the price rise, 1972.

Bury Masco, our felt supplier, did us proud, turning out acre after
acre of different coloured felt for us. Paddington sported coats of green,
light and dark blue, red, brown, purple, and grey, whilst his hats were
even more varied. We can still date a bear by his colour scheme. As our
sales increased, Bury Masco responded, and I was pleased that their

confidence in us when we were starting up ("If we don't look after the smaller customers, how will they ever grow?") was being repaid.

Paddington's all-important feature was his face. He had to have the tip-tilted nose, widely-spaced eyes, and the helpless appealing expression of the original drawings in the books. For years we met so many people who told us how they had viewed a whole shelf full of our bears, but hadn't found the one with the right expression, so had travelled miles to seek others.

I have no recollection of how I made the first bear's body; I probably bought a simplicity pattern from the local Busy Bee and fiddled around with it until I achieved the right shape. As luck would have it, Bury Masco had a large, old, decrepit machine in a back room, which was capable of producing acrylic fur with a woven backing cloth. All fur today has a knitted backing, which means that when you stuff it, it expands indefinitely and loses its shape. The face becomes bloated. Bury Masco's ability to supply *woven-backed* fur was critical in ensuring that our bears kept their shape. It was also good news for Gloria, our loyal contact at Bury Masco. She looked after the vast orders that Gabrielle was placing weekly, nay daily.

From 1972 to 1976 sales grew at an alarming rate. I kept a graph of monthly sales on the wall of the office, which I still have, and it shows that in February 1972 we sold 50 bears, whereas in February 1976 we sold 3,100. The figure for the whole of 1972 was 5,950 bears and for 1976 was 47,750. To cope with this tenfold growth, we had purchased another barn, a stable, a pigsty, the village post office, and a cottage, all around the central fold yard of Home Farm. Wellies were piled high in an outhouse, and rolls of fur were pushed into every available corner. We had a staff of about ten, a small office, four industrial sewing machines and an electric cutter with a vertical blade which went up and down thousands of times a second. The cutter was capable of slicing through forty layers of felt, twelve layers of fur, and as many fingers as you cared to insert with equal ease. As if to prove the last point, one rather stupid uncle of Eddie's was looking round the workroom one day, and thought he would test the sharpness of said blade by running his finger up it. The blade passed the test with flying colours, nearly taking off the end of his finger.

To make Paddington's body, we cut each shape out of thick plastic sheeting, and having layered up the fur, drew round each part. It was a very hit and miss affair because sometimes the template would slip, so the shapes varied in size, but this gave each Paddington individuality.

By knocking two barns into one, we were able to fit in a custom-built table of exactly the same dimensions as a ping-pong table (useful for the children), and Kristina would stay till all hours cutting bodies, heads, arms, legs, hats, and coats, and packing them into boxes to be taken to the outworkers. They consisted of a handful of local housewives who owned domestic sewing machines, and had probably once worked in one of the factories in the town. We had a very good friend who owned a knicker factory, and there was Burtons Tailoring, a massive manufacturer of men's suits quite nearby, and we managed to recruit some of their well trained redundants from time to time.

As you can imagine, Bury Masco were not all that hot on dye lot numbers, the system which classifies rolls of yarn and ensures consistency of colour, so if the arms were cut from one roll, and the bodies from another, chaos resulted in the machine room.

The placing of the eyes was left entirely to chance. Maureen, who had a slight squint, made the holes in PB's face with nail scissors, and where she made them was left to her discretion. There was no template, and certainly no laser-guided beam to guide her! She just jabbed her nail scissors into the cloth. After making the holes, she then inserted the eyes, hammered a metal washer on the shank at the back, and that was that. The nose similarly.

The first real problem as far as the design of Paddington was concerned was his feet. Initially we made his legs as stumps, because it made the cutting and stuffing much easier, and as his feet were encased in Wellingtons we didn't think the stumps would ever be seen. Of course, inquisitive children did pull off the boots and were horrified to discover that their beloved bear was an amputee. In no time at all, we started to receive letters from distraught mothers saying that their children had suffered trauma when removing the boots. They felt their bear had been mutilated. Where were his feet?!

We wrote back, apologising profusely for any distress caused and promising that future Paddingtons would have feet. To the uninitiated, adding feet might seem like the sort of minor adjustment that requires a little tweak to the manufacturing process. Not so. It is easy enough to change the template, but the whole structure of PB's lower torso had to be altered, and the seam now had to run down the centre of his leg, not the side. Besides which, it meant using more fur per bear, and the footpad had to be enlarged, using more felt. When I think about it, my costings were so approximate, that an inch or two more fur really didn't matter. He did look better with feet, and it helps when trying to date a bear; well it would do if I could remember when this change took place.

By 1975 we were drowning, in the best possible sense. Orders were pouring in, almost without us trying, and Eddie realised it was completely unnecessary for him to be driving his BMW the length and breadth of the country visiting customers. His time was better spent in the office, finding overseas agents, signing contracts, and coping with everyday administration. We still had the perfect working relationship:

he handled sales, I handled production, and never the twain should meet. In theory.

In practice, we were both passionate about all aspects of the business and, inevitably, trespassed on each other's territory. Sometimes, this caused conflict. One of the most serious disagreements was about where our bears should be sold. Eddie was very strict about limiting the number of outlets stocking Paddington to one in each town, maybe two in a larger city. He also maintained that if a bookshop, or an undertaker's establishment, or even a fish and chip shop, showed more enthusiasm for Paddington than the local gift or toyshop, then it should have the franchise in that particular town, rather than the more obvious retailer. He also tried to keep the market short, which wasn't difficult in the early days. I was much more short-sighted, and just wanted to sell, sell, sell. The more bears that left the warehouse, the happier I was.

This difference of opinion hardly mattered while demand outstripped supply, as it did for most of the time. We couldn't have flooded the market even if we'd wanted to. But things came to a head when we were approached by Marks and Spencer who wanted to put Paddington in each of their hundreds of stores. I was jumping about with excitement. To my mind, getting our bears into M&S was the ultimate prize, almost an honour. It was the king of the high street at the time, the retailer all other retailers looked up to, and if *it* wanted our bears, we were made!

Eddie had to sit me down, and explain in simple terms the wisdom in his refusal to supply them. M&S would have flooded every town and city in the country with Paddingtons, stretching our production beyond all bounds. Yes, we would have made vast amounts of money, but after one or two seasons, no doubt, they would have changed their allegiance to the Muppets, or Snoopy, or whatever the latest craze happened to be, and we would be left with over-extended premises, too large a workforce, and too much capacity. Most damning of all – no one would want Paddington after he had been so over-exposed. Eddie's great phrase was "You have to starve the market to create the market". With hindsight, of course, he was right.

An even bigger hoo-ha came in about 1978 when Selfridges planned their Christmas windows around different children's characters. Snow White, Cinderella, Pooh, and such like were all there, and right in the middle of Oxford Street there was one window covered in brown paper, reserved, it transpired, for Paddington. Without consulting us, Selfridges had arrogantly assumed that we would supply them.

This wasn't as unreasonable as I make it sound – most gift and soft toy manufacturers would die of ecstasy if Selfridges showed even a smidgen of interest in their product. But we already had a customer in their neighbourhood – Abacus, around the corner in Baker Street – and had given our word to them that no other shop would stock Paddington in that area. We always kept our word, even if it was Selfridges, and even if we could have sold many more bears by breaking it. The row that followed was legendary, involving not just me and Eddie but also Michael Bond and his agent. Michael backed Eddie's decision to turn down Selfridges; Harvey Unna was not so sure. Eddie won the day, and Selfridges had to find something else to put in their Christmas window.

As Paddington took off, we reluctantly stopped production of all our other designs. Tortoises, hedgehogs, Draffakillas, puppets, clowns, cushions and tea cosies all had to go by the board. It was non-stop Paddington Bear.

One problem we faced – I can't imagine it happening these days – was that the electricity supply to Burghwallis became seriously overloaded. We needed three-phase wiring, whatever that means, and the set-up at Home Farm, was not ideal. Eddie and I started to keep an eye out for larger premises. The need became more urgent when in 1976, during the hottest summer on record, we decided in a mad moment to extend the sitting room to accommodate Joanna's baby grand piano. And whilst we were about it, to extend the bedroom above. And make another shower room. Then, why not make a bedroom for Jeremy in the attic, AND replace all the concrete floors with wooden ones. It meant replacing the roof timbers and at one stage we could stand in the cellar, and see the sky. Never mind, we got the piano moved. Perhaps not the best plan in our busiest year, but at least it didn't rain.

Success was also taking its toll on our personal lives. By 1975, Jeremy and Joanna were now at their respective public schools, which meant we had to make long trips to collect them for exeats and then take them back again. The business was all-consuming, the time pressure was intense, and the obvious way to relieve it was to appoint a manageress. We decided there was only one contender for the job: Thelma.

Thelma was a bright, hard-working miner's wife, about 30 years old, an ex-head girl of the local grammar school. The other girls all loved and respected her, and she was the one they went to in times of trouble or if they had any query regarding manufacture. Eddie and I had no doubt at all that her appointment would be a popular one. We decided to break the news one Friday – fish and chip day – and opened a few bottles of champagne ready for a toast. I gathered everyone together and said what a pleasure it was to for me to announce that we had appointed a new manageress – Thelma!

The scenes that followed when I said her name still make me shudder. Insults flew, tempers flared, and plonkers were hurled to the ground. Several girls walked out immediately, including Nora who donned her helmet and revved her motorbike as she sped off. There was a good deal of "verbal", and bit by bit the other girls drifted out, so that twenty minutes after our 'celebratory' announcement the workroom was almost empty – this was just after lunch when it should have been firing on all cylinders. Only a few girls hung back. Kristina, of course, our loyal Polish girl, remained, as did Thelma, who knew which side her bread was buttered. Also, little Maria, a seventeen year old school-leaver, who said she was going nowhere, she loved her job.*

Eddie and I stared at each other, open-mouthed. I don't think we could believe what had happened. We thought that if you gave your staff chips and wine on a Friday, allowed them flexi-time to fit in with their lifestyle, children's holidays and husbands' shifts, paid them a decent wage, and treated them the way you'd like to be treated ourselves, you'd have a happy workforce. In the ensuing months we learned an awful lot about labour relations, and not much of it was pleasant.

As the last girl departed, slamming the door on her way out, the phone rang. It was Hamleys. They had placed an order for three hundred Paddingtons a few weeks previously, and were anxious to know when it would be delivered, as they had a waiting list of impatient customers.

Panic set in.

By coincidence, it was Joanna's first exeat weekend from school, and nothing on God's earth was going to prevent Eddie and me from going down to collect her from Malvern. I cried a good deal of the way down,

---

*Which was a good move for her, as she was later to be appointed as Thelma's successor, after she became a total megalomaniac.

most of it actually, but Eddie said it was a storm in a tea cup, just a bit of jealousy, and when we returned there would be a large bunch of flowers on the doorstep.

There were no flowers, and more importantly there were no girls. Just Thelma, Kristina, Maria, and a machinist called Yvonne, who had been away on the Friday and missed the whole episode. On the workroom floor, little balls of stuffing rolled about in the breeze amongst the empty champagne glasses, plates of cold chips, and discarded plonkers. Where to start?

Eddie rang ACAS (the 'Advisory, Conciliation and Arbitration Service') to get some advice on labour relations, and I set about teaching Betty and our cleaning lady – the indomitable Eunice – how to stuff bears. Neither or them, or me for that matter, had ever stuffed, but three hundred bears were urgently needed and there was no one else to do it. We were advised by ACAS to give the girls an ultimatum: return to work by Wednesday, or consider themselves dismissed, on the grounds that by walking out they had terminated their contracts of employment. Not only did we not have contracts of employment with them; we wouldn't have known what one looked like. Later, we learned just what bad advice ACAS gave us.

On the Tuesday, a meeting was held in one of the girl's houses. Eddie and I went along, confident that they would have cooled down and that we could all be friends again. As I entered the front door, I was actually spat upon – not a good start to the meeting – and when Eddie read the statement from ACAS the arguments of Friday flared up again, and it became quite frightening. These were the same girls, who only days before had sat with me in the garden, laughing, joking, and being as enthusiastic about Paddington as I was. Now they were bitter and acrimonious. Their grouse was mainly based on jealousy: they maintained that there were other potential head girls amongst them and that they should all have been given a chance to apply for the position. We pointed out that had we interviewed all of them, it would have been a waste of time – we would still have chosen Thelma. I suspect it was the increase in Thelma's wages that was really needling them.

Nothing Eddie or I said that evening satisfied them, and we left feeling very demoralised. As we feared, they never returned to work, and the next thing we heard was that they had filed a claim against Gabrielle Designs for unfair dismissal.

The tribunal was held in Sheffield, many months later. I was on crutches – I can't remember why. I think it was DVT. We had retained an eminent QC to put our case, whilst the eight girls turned up unrepresented. Another bad move: tribunals love an underdog.

The trial lasted several days, and I remember Eddie saying, not to worry, it was only a minor blip, and would all blow over, but the headline in that evening's paper – "Shock for Happy Bear Stuffers" – hardly gave us confidence. There then followed a fraught six weeks whilst we waited for the tribunal's ruling (the chairman went on a six-week cruise) using temporary workers to continue production as best we could. We couldn't take on permanent staff in case the tribunal ordered us to re-employ the 'strikers'.

The chairman of the tribunal finally returned, and began by saying that Mr and Mrs Clarkson were amongst the best, kindest, employers he had ever encountered, that we ran a wonderful little company, and treated all the staff like members of the family. Eddie gripped my hand, and whispered, "We've lost". We had. The chairman then continued with an emphatic BUT:

- We hadn't followed the proper guidelines laid down by some department or other.

- We hadn't advertised the position of manager internally.

- We hadn't given the girls long enough time to return to work.

He summed up by saying that all female workers are allowed a few little tantrums every now and then (presumably men just have a damn good punch-up and all is forgotten) and that their walking out did not mean that they had broken their contracts of employment. The blame was apportioned 40/60 in their favour, and a small compensation award was made against us.

After the room cleared, all the girls rushed to embrace us both, tears flowed, and when the chairman returned to collect his papers, he must have wondered why the hell the matter had ever come to court.

There was no time to lick our wounds. Our customers didn't want to know our troubles, they wanted Paddingtons, hundreds of them. Recruiting new girls was easy – the working conditions at Home Farm continued to be superb, especially in the summer when we would spend long hot days, sitting in the sun, stuffing, stitching up, brushing, and dressing bears. There was still wine for lunch on Fridays, and extended coffee breaks. And if there was something good on television, like a royal wedding, or a horse race, we'd all take time out to watch it.

However, even with a full compliment of staff, demand raced ahead of production. Stuffing a bear took about twenty minutes. Coffee breaks or no coffee breaks, we couldn't get enough "plonked" in a day.

About this time we had a call from a children's charity in Doncaster to say that the gorgeous heartthrob, Gerald Harper, was due in the town to present the prize to the winner of a competition. Could we spare some bears? Knowing how Joanna and I drooled every time we watched Gerald on television in *Hadleigh*, Eddie agreed to donate some bears so long as Gerald came to collect them in person. Imagine the excitement that morning in the stuffing room: perfume was sprayed as if from a lawn sprinkler, lip gloss was reapplied every few seconds.

Gerald was fantastic. He discussed every aspect of stuffing with the girls as if it was the most fascinating subject on earth, and even chatted up Eunice, perhaps because she told him he was much bigger than "on the tele". He left with an armful of bears, and an invitation for Joanna, who was away at school and was distraught at missing him, to come down and watch a recording of his Sunday morning radio programme – something to do with handing out roses and champagne. She took up his offer and sat on his knee during the show. God how I envied her!

I don't remember the first time I noticed the derelict transport café on the A1, just north of Doncaster at the famous Red House roundabout, but it must have been some time in 1977, when we were desperate to find new premises. It had the grand name of *Les Routiers*, and no doubt there are still some truckers on the road north out of Doncaster who remember it. The owner had served time in jail, the place had been torched many times, and it was now overrun by rats and the travelling fraternity. Piles of old oil drums, wrecked cars, and Asda trolleys littered the site. The council had obviously given up on it.

To our eyes, it was Shangri-La. It stood on two acres of land, a mile from Burghwallis, on a bus route, within easy reach of three-phase wiring – in fact, the perfect site for a Paddington Bear factory!

We had the building valued at £32,000, but the land on which it stood belonged to the Brodsworth Estate. Brodsworth Hall is a beautiful country house 5 miles to the north-west of Doncaster, now restored to glory by English Heritage, but in the seventies it was in serious disrepair, being inhabited by a wonderful old lady called Mrs

Grant-Dalton. Eddie and I were granted an audience with her to discuss what must have been one of her least valuable property assets.

We were greeted at the door by Griffiths, the faithful old retainer, and escorted into the drawing room. Eddie was wearing his best navy blue suit, which was unfortunate because we sat for an hour on Chippendale chairs upholstered entirely in the dreaded Kapok. The silk long since having worn away from the chair seat, bits of Kapok stuck to his trousers so that when he stood up his bottom resembled a poodle's bum.

Griffiths wheeled in a trolley laden with enough cucumber sandwiches to feed the Brighouse & Rastrick brass band, Madeira cake, warm homemade scones, and strawberry jam, not to mention the silver tea service, complete with strainer, sugar tongs, and Royal Doulton. Mrs Grant-Dalton pressed us to eat. "I never take tea," she said, "but I haven't the heart to tell Griffiths." The Yorkshire terrier then tiddled on the Persian rug, a little hand bell was rung, and the dog removed.

The long and the short of it was that Mrs Grant-Dalton agreed to sell the land to us, and it only remained for us to obtain permission from Doncaster Planning Authority to use the building as a factory. Anticipating no problem on that front – the chief planning officer was, after all, a Rotarian colleague of my father's – we went ahead and bought the place. The planning officer had already visited the site and been very amenable, saying he "couldn't imagine a more acceptable application". He agreed that it had been a thorn in the council's side for long enough, and a small industrial unit emitting no evil smells, no noise, and providing employment to local ladies was ideal.

We were refused permission.

Reasons of some sort were given. There were mutterings about the importance of preserving the green belt, and they even had the gall to cite 'increased traffic' as one of the points against our application. Given that the Red House's most recent use had been as a transport café, this was laughable. We suspected that the decision had more to do with the fact that Eddie had stood as Conservative candidate in the local elections than anything else, but perhaps that is too cynical. Anyway, we decided to appeal, but in the meantime to carry on as if we *had* been granted permission because there was no time to be lost.

Builders were hired (ironically, the husbands of our walker-outers!) to convert the premises into a factory and they did a fantastic job. It was a Herculean task. The kitchen of the transport café had housed a large fat fryer, and after it closed the local yobbos had let all the rancid fat out on to the floor, giving the rats a field day. They had then let off all the fire extinguishers, lit bonfires, smashed windows, and filled the lavatories.

Luckily for us, this was the time of the new development of a fly-over at the notorious Red House roundabout on the A1. The contractors, needing a site for their equipment and offices etc., asked if they could use our land, and in lieu of rent, offered to landscape the whole area, plant trees, and put up fencing. We agreed. All this work, together with the renovation of the interior, took about 6 months. Then we named it The Bear Garden. Little did we know how significant that name would be in the years to come.

The workrooms at Home Farm were relocated to The Bear Garden, and the factory finally whirred into action. For the time being, the administrative side of Gabrielle stayed at Home Farm.

Our manufacturing techniques were transformed by the move to The Bear Garden, because we were able to install a proper stuffing machine. A monstrous beast, it consisted of a drum housing large paddles, which churned up the stuffing and forced it out by compressed air, through two pipes, into the bears. Paddington had these pipes shoved ignominiously up his bum. The carcass was filled in about three minutes, a great improvement on the old plonking method. Kapok had long since been replaced by other stuffing known as G5 – not to be confused with G6. Put G6 in your machine, and it clogs. Not a lot of people know that (or care).

The Bear Garden after our landscaping.

On a recent visit to Hamleys I saw that they had installed one of these machines in the soft toy department, and the young girl who was stuffing a horrendous bear for my granddaughter was sweetly telling me how the machine worked. I never said a word!

Using the stuffing machine was exhausting work, noisy too, so the girls would take turns to stuff twenty bears, then fill the joints to make them firm, sew up the orifice, and finally pile them up for the finishing process. Each bear would be brushed and given a whack on his nose. This may sound stupid, but there was no doubt – the whack gave him that appealing tip-tilted look.

The sewing room at The Bear Garden housed eight or nine industrial sewing machines, which turned out all the skins, coats and hats. Bury Masco were flat out producing hundreds of metres of felt, and their one antiquated machine was occupied full-time weaving the fur.

Even with all this modern machinery, turning out up to 1,500 bears a week, we struggled to cope with the demand. The next step was to start a twilight shift. A dozen or so local ladies would put their children to bed, leave their husbands to babysit, and come to work, well into the night, bringing with them homemade cakes, custard pies, and the odd tiramisu. They had a veritable midnight feast every night. Completely unsupervised they managed to produce a table full of 100 bears in every shift, so that when the day staff arrived they could immediately start dressing and packing.

Of course, all this time we were living with a shadow over our heads and, sure enough, the knock came on the door. The official-looking man in a trilby standing there asked me what went on at The Bear Garden (as if he didn't know!) I said it was a bear factory. He told me to stop production immediately. I said that I was sorry but I couldn't. He said I must, and before leaving, handed me an enforcement notice. Which, of course, we ignored.

Eddie and I reasoned that it would take at least two years for the planning authority to put us out on the footpath if we appealed against every decision. Two years is a long time – we could make a lot of bears in that time. If the planners really wanted a fight, they could have one, but we'd square up to them at the last possible moment.

In the meantime, another problem surfaced, and again it was in the thorny area of labour relations which had so hurt us before. In our rush to get the new factory up and running, we recruited lots of staff, and were less than scrupulous when it came to checking references. In fact

I don't remember asking for references from anyone. One woman who slipped through the net was Sharon. She was a militant trade unionist and came armed with a stopwatch, a thermometer, and a pile of health and safety rulebooks, referring to all of them at regular intervals.

Despite our run-in with the industrial tribunal, Eddie and I were still terribly naïve when it came to dealing with our employees. We abided by the principle that if you treated them in a civilised way, they would be happy to work for you, and that it doesn't matter whether you obey the letter of employment law as long as you obey the spirit. So, we allowed our staff to take regular breaks in hot weather, we bought them ice-creams and cold drinks, we never had a clocking-on machine, and we never made checks on individual productivity. We trusted them and felt that as long as people were doing their best, speeds were bound to vary between one worker and the next. As for quality control – there wasn't any! They all knew what a bear should look like, and anyway, Thelma was that control!

This casual approach to employee relations seemed to work well, but was brought to an abrupt halt by the actions of Sharon. She was bad news. A few weeks after starting work with us, she went off for thirteen weeks "sick leave". On her return to work one Monday morning, she announced that she was now the new union leader. She had recruited a small number of the other girls to the TGWU, and in future, she said, all work policies in the factory would be dictated by her. She had even obtained a set of our company accounts from Companies House, and distributed copies around the local colliery where her husband worked.

The effect of all this stirring was immediate and profound. Every coffee break became an ad hoc union meeting, and in place of the usual raucous laughter, the banter, and the gossip, there were long dissertations on the evils of Gabrielle Designs and its unscrupulous bosses. It was alleged that we were making more profit than Burton Tailoring – considering they went bust within the year this was probably not far from the truth. When our company accounts were circulated to the girls in the factory, we invited Sharon to read the document to them out loud, explaining each entry as she did so. It was only a single sheet, and in abbreviated form, so it said very little about the company's real financial state, but Eddie and I thought that if we were being painted as greedy capitalists, we should at least know what the charges were!

As Sharon read out the figures it became clear that she understood hardly any of the entries – her definition of "depreciation" was "people not saying thank you". She further admitted that she couldn't read a balance sheet. She's not the only one.

Things got worse. The local secretary of the TGWU, a weasel-faced ginger-top who I will call Mr G. rang us to say that he wanted to come and talk to the girls. We didn't refuse, but invited him to first visit us for a cup of tea at Home Farm. He loved our house, and said it reminded him of his own little cottage high up in a Pennine village. "Only for use at the weekends you understand," he said cryptically. We ushered him politely into the sitting room and brought in the tea. Before his arrival Jeremy had rigged up a portable tape-recorder under Eddie's chair, the tape was set, and all Eddie had to do was press the record button at the strategic moment.

The conversation plummeted rapidly from discussion of such niceties as the weather, into Mr G.'s future plans for Gabrielle Designs. *His* future plans, mind! Complete unionisation was the gist of it, whilst complete rejection was ours. Now this evil little toad had learned from our MP that our refused planning application was going to appeal. He played his ace card, implying that if we refused to become unionised, he would make it difficult for us to obtain planning application.

Eddie had realised that negotiations were becoming heated, and nonchalantly leaned back in his chair to press that all important record button, but like me he was useless at anything even slightly electronic, and he pressed rewind instead. Unmistakable reverse-tape noises could be heard coming from the chair but our fat little friend didn't seem to notice, and the argument raged on. He left after demanding to talk to all the girls on the factory site.

A few days later, we all assembled in The Bear Garden's new canteen, a beautiful, bright room on the first floor, with panoramic views across South Yorkshire. It was painted primrose, with new white tables and chairs, and equipped with a cooker, a microwave, and a radio. Mr G. objected at first to Eddie and me being present, but little Maria, who had stuck to her guns so faithfully in the walk-out, announced that if Mr and Mrs Clarkson worked alongside them on the factory floor, then they had every right to remain.

There followed one of the most humiliating experiences of our lives. Today, being more experienced at dealing with horrid people, I would no doubt have thumped him. He publicly revealed our salaries, he denigrated us as people and bosses, he likened us to Victorian fathers who patronisingly patted the heads of their children, as we handed out their weekly wages – "mere pittances", as he described them, "way below the standard rate". This was nonsense. We always paid the going rate or higher, and we also paid staff enormous bonuses at Christmas each year. One year they each received £400 – a lot of money in the seventies – and we took everyone to a beautiful banqueting hall in York where, at each seat there was a bottle of brandy and a new Paddington 'Beanie'.

Maria defended us by reminding everyone about the Christmas bonuses. Mr G. retorted by asking the assembled group if they trusted us to continue paying such amounts, and said everyone who did *not* trust us should put up their hand. It was some solace that only Sharon and her best friend put them up.

Eddie then played his joker. He reminded Mr G. of the meeting we had had at Home Farm, and of his threat to scupper our planning permission for the factory. A hush went round the room. The girls may have been susceptible to his claims that they were being exploited, but the last thing any of them wanted was to see the business close and their jobs lost. All eyes turned on Mr G.

Silence.

Eddie then reminded him of the whirring noise under his chair. Mr G. looked perplexed.

"That was a tape recorder recording your threat," he lied.

Mr G. went the colour of beetroot. He knew he was cornered. Shoving his papers into his briefcase and without so much as a by-your-leave, he fled from the room, and nothing more was ever heard of him.

Victory!

Sadly, not a complete one. We might have got rid of Mr G. but we were still stuck with Sharon, the witch, and she was still on wrecking duty. If the temperature in the factory rose by one degree, she demanded cold drinks all round, and a walk round the cherry tree. If it fell by one degree, it was too cold to work, and everyone had to go home. If her machine needed moving six inches, a man had to be employed to move it. Every trick in the union book was deployed.

In the months that followed, life became unbearable. The happy work atmosphere that had existed before was shattered. We were losing sleep, and Eddie's inhaler was being used more than his cigarette lighter. I vowed to rid us of the evil monster responsible, if I had to drag her by her cardy to the Sheffield Tribunal, and demand "How much?"

One morning, I decided I would do it. I arrived at the factory, hell bent on dismissing Sharon, to find her waiting outside my office door, resignation letter in hand!! I couldn't believe my luck. Her departure was like a can of air freshener being sprayed into the factory. Smiles reappeared, production increased, and we became a happy little band once more.

Whilst all this was going on, we were slightly concerned about our appeal against the refusal of planning permission on the factory. It was a distraction we could have done without. I didn't really want to waste time fighting councils. I just wanted to get on with the job of ordering the fur, the wellies, the eyes and noses, and the stuffing for our bears. With sales going like the clappers, we couldn't afford to have production held up for lack of supplies. Nor could we continue to collect second-hand cartons from the rear of supermarkets; we had to buy in custom-sized boxes, in very large quantities, which took into account the height restrictions for certain export markets. The boxes also had to be tamper-proof, because if the carriers knew the contents were Paddingtons – very saleable items on the black market – the risk of pilferage was high.

To strengthen our appeal against the planning refusal, we organised a local petition, signed by thousands, in support of allowing us to continue working in The Bear Garden. The hearing was in Doncaster, on the hottest August day I ever remember. Once again we had briefed a London QC, who attended in a pin-striped suit with a stiff white collar and rosebud in the button hole. We met him first at the factory. It was Eunice's ironing day and being no respecter of authority, she shouted to him as he went down the drive, "You're just in time to finish t'ironing. I've saved y'knickers!"

21st June, 1976

PETITION APPEAL

We, Gabrielle Designs Limited of Burghwallis decided to expand our business, into the dis-used, dirty and derelict transport cafe known as "Les Routiers", Red House Corner, Woodlands which had gone bankrupt two years earlier. We did this after first consulting the Planning Department and our local Councillor, both stating that they considered the "change of use" very desirable. As you are probably aware the Doncaster Metropolitan Borough Council Technical Services Department have now twice refused to allow the "change of use" and their reasons are that the building is in the Green Belt and that land is available on industrial estates.

Our one and only product, Paddington Bear, is in great demand throughout the whole world. Such is the demand that we have found it absolutely necessary to move into our new "home". We cannot wait for new work rooms to be planned and built as jobs and exports are at stake. This move has brought with it more job opportunities and a real chance of increasing our export markets NOW. We believe that we shall improve the site enormously, that a "change of use" to light industrial premises is much more desirable in a Green Belt than a derelict transport cafe with day and overnight parking by lorries, gypsies etcetera. We have promised to landscape the site with grass, shrubs, trees and at no cost to the rate payer.

My wife and I have been so much encouraged in our efforts by the many people who have telephoned, written, and stopped us in the street to give their support. We now need the support of many more local people at the Public Enquiry to be held at Nether Hall on July 6th 1976.

IF WE LOSE THIS APPEAL LOCAL JOB OPPORTUNITIES AND EXPORTS WILL BE LOST.

WILL YOU PLEASE HELP by signing this letter in support of our effort.
Yours very sincerely,
GABRIELLE DESIGNS

Edward G. Clarkson

Signed ....
Address ....
Would you kindly sign and return to your newsagent or to your newspaper boy, or to the person who handed it to you.

ASKEW PRINTERS, DONCASTER.

A copy of the petition to get planning permission for The Bear Garden, 1976.

I was keen to make a good impression on him, and, knowing only too well the dearth of decent hostelries in Doncaster, I went to enormous pains to make a Fortnum-style hamper, which we could take to the local municipal park when the court broke for lunch. I laid on asparagus rolls, smoked salmon sandwiches, fresh raspberries and cream, and a very expensive bottle of Chablis. These couldn't be left in the car boot all morning in those temperatures, so I bribed the butcher next to the council chambers to store the lot in his fridge. I could swear I didn't say 'freezer'!!

The morning hearing went well. Our QC appeared to be quietly humiliating the little bearded solicitor from the council, who I remember was sweating a lot, but then we all were.

We adjourned for lunch at one o'clock. Eddie ushered our QC to an air-conditioned car, whilst I picked up the picnic from the butchers. We perched on the only available park bench, just outside the gent's loo. (I never realised, until I joined the magistrates bench five years later, what a notorious loo it was.) The memory of opening that hamper, and listening to our QC crunching his way through frozen asparagus rolls, and hacking at the cream with a knife to put on his crispy raspberries will remain with me to my dying day. And guess what? We had forgotten the bottle opener.

Back in the council chamber, the afternoon seemed to go even better than the morning. We established that the boundary line which delineated the green belt had been moved by the council specifically to include our site, the local residents in attendance thumped their fists on the tables, and we were confident permission would be granted. The chairman remained stony faced, giving nothing away, and suggested we all took a trip to the site. I drove, making jaunty little quips as we went. We showed him what a fantastic job we had already made of the site, and then put him on the train to King's Cross.

We lost the appeal.

It was a terrible blow, but we couldn't dwell on it. We asked our lawyer to summarise what our legal options were now, then we got back to running the business. The latest production bottleneck was in the cutting department, where we cut Paddington's clothes. They just couldn't cut enough to keep up with the rest of the factory. By a stroke of luck, a salesman made a cold call on The Bear Garden, and as was my wont, I sent him packing – I was far too busy to see anyone. As he started up his car I glanced at the literature he had left behind, let out a piercing shriek, rushed out, grabbed him, and ordered a £3,000 cutting machine on the spot. I think in today's money that is around £100,000. It was a fantastic piece of equipment, a six-foot wide lump of steel. The fabric could be laid up many layers deep on a table behind the machine, as before, and as it was pulled under the machine head you could insert any shape of die cutter (rather like pastry cutters, but made from pressed steel), then bring twelve tons of pressure down with a clonk, cutting whatever shape you wanted. All bear parts, heads, arms, legs, and bodies were precision cut. We even had the eye sockets pierced. Each die cost hundreds or even thousands of pounds, and then there were all the parts of hats and coats. Fortunately, it was impossible to get your head under the machine, or even your hands, because you needed both of them to operate it, but occasionally foreign objects were left in the wrong place, and it took no prisoners, cutting clean through bell metal. We had come a long way from that first circle cutter for the hens' eyes.

It was just as well that we did install that cutting machine, because sales continued at a fantastic pace throughout 1978. We averaged about 5,000 bears per month that year, and in two of them we made more than 10,000. Our all-time production record was 11,500, in November. The workforce was content, loyal, dedicated, and hard working. We moved the office up to The Bear Garden, and had two wonderful ladies

– Joan and Irene – to deal with the orders, wages, invoices, and VAT returns. There was a buxom lady to make the coffee and lunches, and Sid in the storeroom pulled endless rolls of fur and felt through to the cutting room.

When I look back on the people we employed, I think we must have had a monopoly of eccentric, wonderful, interesting, weird, dodgy – nay, in some cases corrupt – characters in the area. The description of us on the Paddington labels as 'the craftswomen of Yorkshire' was only half the story. There was Jean, who had an obsession with ric-rac braid; Moira who the rest of us thought was running a catalogue, but who was in fact shoplifting to order – she could get you anything from cashmere to a video recorder at a knockdown price. There was Pauline, who couldn't work with fur "cause it makes me itch"; Beryl who said she had fourteen O-levels, and that her brother was doing time for manslaughter. Alice had to go home for the day whenever she saw a dead cat on her way to work, and had a (perhaps not unrelated) hobby of growing cannabis in her garden. Mavis couldn't stuff if it was thundering, and dear little Maria, the sixteen year-old who stuck with us during the infamous walk-out – her Yorkshire speak was a language all of its own. When asked by Eddie to go and fetch a document from the biscuit tin in which we kept items of importance, she came back empty-handed and announced "Tint in tin". This quickly became a catch phrase at Gabrielle.

Eunice, of course, was our most incorrigible. She was a divorcee with a handful of beautiful daughters, and a devoted mother who didn't like her kids going off to school on snowy mornings. One day she left one of the girls, Donna, asleep at home while she came to work. This wasn't so unusual except that it was the day that Donna was due to sit her one and only O-level. "Never mind," said Eunice when her distraught daughter phoned, "they'll let you take it on Monday."

What Eunice could never understand was why she couldn't work and also receive unemployment benefit. It wasn't the ethical issue that she struggled with, but the practical one. I tried to explain that she was in our books so if she also claimed benefit she would get caught out. Her answer to that was simple: just tear the page out with her name on it. When I said we couldn't do that she replied that the Inland Revenue would never connect her with the employment office, because all her mail had 'Private and Confidential' on it. And if the authorities did pay her a visit, she said, she would hang her raggy old curtains in the windows, replacing the rich velvet ones after they'd gone. Thus would they be fooled!

We loved Eunice dearly, so much so that when the family went on holiday she would come in daily to spring clean and keep an eye on things. Our affection for her would have been tested if she had carried out her idea to paint different colours between the beams in our kitchen whilst we were away. As it was, we never knew in which room we would find the television when we came home – she loved re-arranging the house for us. Her ex-husband had been a miner, and every Friday night would come home to say he had lost his wage packet. Poor gullible Eunice would spend the evening searching the streets for it.

Our neighbours were never dull either. Apart from the aforementioned Mrs H., who tried to close us down, we had a chef next door, called Bob Hope. Honestly. He was stopped by the police one night after a fancy dress party, dressed in sequins from head to toe, and was asked to give his name.

Then there was the sex maniac in the cottage below who ran around the garden naked. She definitely needed ironing. Her husband collected Alvis cars, and after he died, she had regular visits from a mechanic who drove a white van packed with tools, had a gap between his teeth, and travelled around the whole of Yorkshire on the job. We became convinced that he was the Yorkshire Ripper, and even mentioned him to a police friend of ours, who pointed out that that if he didn't have a Geordie accent he couldn't be the mass rapist and murderer. Joanna was at Leeds University at the time of the Ripper, doing the first of her degrees, and living in the Headingley district. We became so worried after the murder of Jacqueline Hill, in Headingley in 1980, that we bought a small Volvo, and said she could have the use of it until the bastard was caught. That seemed safer than walking or using public transport, but in fact the car was so unreliable that she was in far more danger from breaking down at night and being stranded at the roadside. Thankfully, in January 1981, Peter Sutcliffe was caught. Joanna, destined to be a lawyer, argued that she should keep the car because he might appeal!

Other strange characters popped into our lives on an ad hoc basis. We employed a builder to carry out some conversion work which involved breaking into the workroom's drainage from the lavatory. He never informed us for a week, and when I found him standing in his wellies, he said it didn't matter, because he knew it was only women who used that loo.

Looking back it seems extraordinary that we managed to produce a single Paddington Bear, let alone the tens of thousands that we were selling by the late seventies. Michael's books had been translated into twenty-six languages, and sat on library shelves from Alice Springs to Alaska. We were sending bears to Japan, Australia, France, Germany, Bermuda, New Zealand and Scandinavia, usually through agents who we had appointed in the various markets.

Eddie greatly enjoyed visiting the European agents, particularly those in countries with good food. I remember him returning from Tourcoing on the French-Belgian border where he had been royally entertained by a Monsieur Florin, our French agent. Their business discussions had been lubricated by dozens of oysters and numerous gallons of champagne. Eddie paid the price for his gluttony, not being able to move from his bed for four days. In fact he nearly died (again)!

Our Australian agent, whose name I've forgotten, ran a company called Wump. She was a gorgeous girl standing over six feet tall, weighed about two stone, and could have been a model if she hadn't caught the Paddington bug. She flew over to visit us regularly, hand-picked her bears, and had them shipped out naked, with all their clothes packed separately. When they arrived down under, she would press each hat and coat, dress the bears, and drive them in her station wagon to various shops around Australia! How she made a profit, we never understood.

Of course, the biggest potential market overseas was America. This was the one which, if it took off, would eclipse all other markets. We knew that, Michael Bond and his agents knew that, and as the whole Paddington phenomenon gathered pace, the question of America hung in the air. Contractually, Gabrielle Designs had world rights so we could, if we had wanted, have insisted on "taking on America" ourselves. The reality, however, was that we had no experience of the American market, no contacts there, and our production capacity was already stretched to breaking point.

Not selling Paddington Bears into the world's biggest market was simply not an option. Reluctantly, we agreed to a revised contract with Michael Bond's Paddington Company, in which we relinquished all our overseas rights to a company in America. The largest toy company in the world actually – Eden Toys Inc., New York We retained our UK rights and received royalties from Eden on non-UK sales. Looking back, it was the only possible solution to the problem of production, but in a way we felt we had failed.

Inevitably, our relationship with Eden Toys was a tense one. They were a vast multinational, with profit targets to hit and shareholders to please, who manufactured on an industrial scale. We were a small UK operation, privately owned, which existed (at least partly) because we loved our products and had a lot of fun making them. Eden and Gabrielle were like oil and water.

At their request, I sent all my patterns over to the States, but Eden decided to do things their own way, using different production methods, with the result that their PB never quite had the same Paddington expression as ours. At least, that was my opinion. And when you think about it, how could it have been any other way? They didn't have a Gloria, or a Bury Masco, or a Mr Ormerod over there. I'm sure their eyes were inserted by machine, and their fur had a knitted backing which distorted on stuffing, making the poor chap look like he was on steroids.

I suspect there was an even deeper reason though: we had always thought of Paddington as a living, loving, breathing bear, whereas Eden referred to him as having a merchantable rate.

Chapter Eight – Highs and Lows

It was my birthday, November 9th 1977, when we heard the news that planning consent for The Bear Garden had at long last been granted. Apparently our application had gone all the way to the House of Lords and had been rejected AGAIN! They really didn't want us did they? When all seemed lost Peter Shore, a government minister, stepped in and overruled the Lords' decision on the grounds that Gabrielle Designs was making an important contribution to the export drive.

I suppose this was a momentous day for us, but we really didn't have time to think about it, let alone celebrate. The only thing we had time for was producing bears. If I am ever asked to advise young entrepreneurs today, I will say, stop for one moment and consider how your obsession with work can affect those around you, because there *is* a price to pay for business success. Friends become slightly wary of you and stop ringing because they think you're too busy to talk, which you generally are. They don't drop in to see you because they assume you'll be at work, which you usually are. And you become very boring at dinner parties, because your business is just about the only thing you can talk about. And you do.

At the time Eddie and I didn't really notice these things happening to us, but looking back there is no doubt that they were, and I regret that.

Later, in the early eighties, Eddie and I lost some good friends through a simple misunderstanding. We had been holidaying in Dorset, and happened to come across a gorgeous shop in Wareham called 'The House of Bears'. The couple who ran it, Mr and Mrs Hildesley, invited us in to look around even though they were closed. Mary Hildesley made hundreds of bears, about six inches high, each one dressed as a different character, each one handmade and dressed entirely in hand-knitted outfits. The house was laid out like a country mansion with a kitchen, a parlour, an office, a nursery, a playroom, a dining room, and outside there were stables, a walled gardens, and a greenhouse. Inside each room was the appropriate collection of bear characters: cooks in the kitchen, nannies in the bedroom, a clergyman in the drawing room, grooms in the stables, and gardeners tending the flower beds. There were mothers nursing babies, and even the babies had hand-knitted shawls. All the ladies' hats were perfect in every detail, all the flowers were knitted. It was a wonderful fantasy world, executed with flair and imagination.

Eddie and I were instantly captivated, as anyone would have been. We told Mary of our connection with Paddington and hit it off straight away. Addresses were exchanged and a very special bond developed between us.

Part of their enormous bear collection was a team of rugby players called, naturally, 'The Barbearians', who sported red and white (knitted) jerseys. No 4 was called 'Scrum', and he had a girl friend called 'Scrum's Girlfriend' because apparently she changed so often that no one could remember her name. Such was their humour. When we invited the

Hildesleys to come and stay with us, they brought us a Scrum Bear as a gift.

It was about this time that we decided to bring out Paddington in another outfit. The options were limited. Apart from PB's wellies. pyjamas and dressing gown, the only other clothing mentioned by Michael Bond in the books was his rugby kit. We discussed the idea of a rugby Paddington with Michael and the more we discussed it, the more we liked it. It would be faithful to the books, it would be new, and it would appeal to rugger buggers and their girlfriends. One of the disadvantages of the teddy bear market is that the products tend to be bought only by women, because men regard it as a blow to their manhood to own something so cute. But a teddy bear dressed in rugby kit is different. It is macho enough to be an acceptable present to a man, thus doubling the potential market! We didn't usually think in such mercenary terms, but we were in business and it was a factor.

Having made the decision to go ahead with a rugby Paddington, I immediately got stuck in. The first dilemma was what colour jersey to put him in. It was no good putting him in Gloucester's club shirt, because that would put off buyers who supported other clubs. Ditto Leicester Tigers. Ditto Bath. The only solution was to get him *all* the main team strips. Leicester is of course famous for producing knitted fabrics, so off I went, with a list of every combination of stripes: red and white, blue and white, green and white, red green and white (Leicester Tigers!), black and white, black and red, etc. We even tackled the awkward quartered design of Harlequins. In all, we needed seventeen different colour ways, and each one had to be hundreds of metres long.

Great in the ruck, but no good at converting.

The shorts were either black or white – no problem. The boots had to have studs and 'PB' stamped on the sole, but a couple of thousand for a new mould would fix that, and we could punch the lace holes in ourselves and then thread in some laces. He also had a sports bag containing spare shorts, a headband, etc. In a few months we had Paddington fully equipped for his sporting activities and began planning his launch to the market.

At the NEC Gift Fair in 1980 we took a big stand and set it out as a rugby pitch. There were tall rugby posts at each end, and an entire scrum of bears on the pitch, each wearing a different coloured strip. At the side we had seating, and on the seats we put all our other products, forming the crowd.

Having spent all day setting this up, we went back to our hotel exhausted, but delighted with the final result. Next morning we arrived at the stand to find Mr Hildesley waiting with one of his Scrum Bears in his hand. It was obvious something was wrong. He was purple with rage, and let forth a string of abuse. He accused Eddie and me of stealing his wife's design and blatantly using it for Paddington. How, he asked, could we abuse their friendship in this way, after they had shown us such kindness?

I was stunned. I simply didn't agree that our bear was a rip-off of their design. As I tried to explain to him, Mary made bears in every conceivable outfit. It wouldn't have mattered what we dressed Paddington in, she would have had a similar character.

There was no placating him. He said Mary was devastated, and never wanted to speak to us again. They never did.

That all happened in the eighties, so I'm getting ahead of myself. Back in the late seventies we were also launching new products – mainly accessories for Paddington, and the dilemma we faced every time was how big a production run to do. Suppliers offer better terms for large quantities, so the temptation is to "go large" in order to reduce the production costs, but the trouble is, this increases risk. If the product fails, you're left with a load of unsellable stock.

We faced this problem time and again. For example, in 1977 we introduced pyjamas for Paddington, which were sold separately, and retailed at £2.80. I wanted the flannelette for these to exactly match the pyjamas he wore in the TV series which was broadcast at the time, hideous though it was: orange, purple, and brown flowers. At last my textile training came into use. Off I went to Lancashire to find a manufacturer of flannelette who was willing to print the ghastly stuff. I found one, can't remember who it was, but I do remember that the minimum quantity that they would print was 75,000 yards, which equated to 75,000 pairs of pyjamas! I must have been feeling very confident about the business, because I placed the order. To this day I still have a couple of bolts under the kitchen sink – it makes brilliant polishing cloths.

We followed the pyjamas with a dressing gown, complete with PB embroidered on the pocket, and there were other accessories too. Eddie really enjoyed designing the promotional leaflets for these add-ons. For the pyjamas and dressing gown we had a photograph of PB in full caboodle, with a caption underneath saying, "In and out of bed, still the smartest bear".

The mid to late seventies were our golden years. In our best year, 1978, the sales were:

1978	Bears
January	5,850
February	5,100
March	6,800
April	4,750
May	6,600
June	5,500
July	9,250
August	6,800
September	8,500
October	10,600
November	11,500
December	5,750

The Paddington phenomenon was at its height, with branded products of all types coming out. As well as our bears, there was a range of stationery, sheets and bedding, and ceramic giftware. Two 'Paddington and Friends' retail shops opened in London and Bath, and a Paddington TV show was broadcast on BBC One.

The Paddington BBC show was, to my mind, a masterpiece. The designer was Ivor Wood, a brilliant artistic creator from Yorkshire (of course). He used a miniature Paddington no more than 6 or 7 inches high, but every joint was a brass ball and socket, even in his nose. I think the filming process is known as 'freeze frame', and it must have taken hours and hours to do, moving the bear a fraction of an inch at a time. All the backgrounds were exquisite two-dimensional drawings, making Paddington stand out as the central figure. The voiceover was by Michael Hordern.

All these ventures helped each other. Gabrielle Designs had become well known in the trade, Eddie and I did numerous TV interviews, Hamleys posted a large notice by its door saying 'Paddington Bear on the fourth floor', and one year Paddington was even voted 'Toy of the Year'. Whatever people tell you about the downside of success, it is wonderfully satisfying when it happens, particularly if you've worked hard for it. Eddie and I certainly enjoyed ourselves, and there were benefits for our children too – Jeremy's sex life was transformed for one. He could get a dance/snog with any girl at Abbots Bromley just by promising her a PB.

Other highlights:

- Princess Anne was photographed coming out of hospital after the birth of Zara with the Sister holding a Paddington Bear which had been presented to her.

- Torville and Dean used PB as their mascot. He often featured on the conveyor belt in *The Generation Game* provoking those moronic shrieks of "cuddly toy!", and Twiggy posed with him.

- When HM The Queen visited Doncaster to meet some prominent business people in the town, I had the honour of being presented to her, and she was presented with a Paddington. When she visited a second time in 1994 to celebrate the 800th anniversary of Doncaster being granted a royal charter by King John, I actually had a chat with her, and apologised for not bringing her another bear. (We were out of stock.)

- When the British and French engineers finally completed the digging of the Channel Tunnel in 1991, after the initial handshake, a Paddington Bear was passed through to the French side, as a symbol of friendship. (My God it would take more than a bear to unite the two countries today! Especially one dressed in rugby gear.)

Twiggy where did you get that fur? © The Press Association Ltd.

There was a Japanese TV company, Akai Enterprises, which decided that Gabrielle Designs would make an ideal subject for a quiz show. Their idea was to come over to the factory, film Paddington being made, and then ask the children back in Japan questions about the process. One question was "What do the ladies at Gabrielle do to Paddington?" Another was "What legal contract has to be negotiated before the merchandise can be put on the market?" which was a bit tricky for seven year-olds, I thought. The answer to the first question was "They bash him on the nose". The second, I couldn't answer!

The film crew arrived one morning, none of them speaking a word of English except for the director. He translated the story of Paddington as I told it to the reporter in the outfit, who took it all down in Japanese shorthand. We told him about the various sizes, prices, and background history of Gabrielle Designs, and made a special point of stressing that we had exclusive copyright, because we were worried about an enterprising Japanese pirating our design.

When we told them about Aunt Lucy, they asked where were Paddington's mother and father. I explained that he didn't have any parents. "What has happened to them?" enquired Mr Akai, alarmed. I said that he had never had any. "Ah so, he is as Mary in the Bible." My God! I thought, he thinks Paddington is a virgin birth! We've probably started a whole new religious cult in Japan, they think the Messiah has been reborn here in Doncaster, wearing Wellington boots, we shall have pilgrimages coming to the town! That would put the St. Leger in the shade!

Early in 1978, I decided to design a mini Paddington, a sort of cross between a pram adornment and an executive toy for upmarket desks. He was a small bean bag, had to have much shorter fur, didn't wear boots, and was designed to look fat and irresistibly cuddly. I took Beanie, as he was known, down to visit Michael for his approval. I placed him on the desk, and we both sat in silence for a full five minutes. Michael said not a word, but just turned him around, picked him up, prodded him, and eventually gave a wry smile, which was the equivalent of saying "Crack on!" Phew! What a relief.

There were, however, two caveats. Firstly, Michael was concerned that if the duffle coat did not fasten up properly, Paddington might look like a flasher exposing himself – not an image we really wanted to portray. Secondly, when he learned that we had filled Beanie with split peas, Michael said that there was far too much hunger in the world for Paddington to be filled with an edible product. He was right of course. We found a substitute in some polystyrene beads, and with the aid of a plastic tooth mug and a funnel, they could be poured in the correct quantity into his long-suffering orifice.

We had to have Beanie's eyes and nose specially made at a plastic extrusions firm in Oxford – once again, by the million – and the washers specially made by an engineering works in Birmingham. Two vastly expensive sewing machines were purchased, which, at a stroke, automatically sewed on the tiny pockets and tabs. A wood turner in the wilds of North Yorkshire made the toggles, no more than 5mm long, and they were sewn on by a machine similar to the one that stitches buttons on for Marks and Spencer: one pull of a thread and the whole lot comes undone.

I really enjoyed travelling around the country sourcing components from suppliers. I had a very smart executive grey greatcoat, an impressive briefcase, drove a large albeit ugly Volvo Estate, and usually stayed in rather smart hotels. If I took my briefcase into the dining room and made notes during dinner, I could be guaranteed fantastic attention from the head waiter, and once, at the Lygon Arms in the Cotswolds, after making a mild complaint about too much lemon on the scampi, I had dinner, bed and breakfast for free. It was Eddie who pointed out that they obviously thought I was an inspector from Egon Ronay.

The actual stitching of Beanie's skins proved too difficult for our machinists at that time, but we struck gold when we found Martin.

Another charismatic person, he was an ex-public school son of a millionaire pram manufacturer. His father had long since given up on him, so he had started his own manufacturing business in Guisborough, North Yorkshire. It was housed in a ramshackle windowless building, full of grubby-fingered machinists, an enormous Irish wolfhound, and a great aunt in her nineties who humped around the large rolls of cloth. In the corner stood a gramophone, which blared out old cracked 78s. Martin's desk was a trestle table littered with unpaid invoices and empty dog-meat tins. Just our sort of man! We gave him a contract to make the mini skins immediately.

When I first visited Martin's works, the floor was covered with huge piles of 'Roly Rabbits'. These were large fluffy white rabbits with tartan ears, a tail, and a tartan bow round their necks. It was the era of The Bay City Rollers, the Scottish pop group of the mid-seventies, and Martin had tried to take advantage of 'Rollermania'. Unfortunately, he never quite thought things through; he didn't realise that the fans were all under fourteen, and that Roly Rabbit retailed at a price that was way out of their pocket money range.

Undaunted, he cut off Roly Rabbit's ears and tail, removed his bow, and replaced them with yellow and blue, the Leeds United colours. That was the year that Leeds were knocked out of the cup in the first round.

Martin would quite happily admit to other disasters. One year he went heavily into towelling shell suits, advertising them at enormous cost in the Sunday supplements. He guaranteed delivery within 21 days, which would have been fine except that his advert didn't appear until December 10th.

It's always more fun hearing about people's business mistakes than their successes, and you can learn much more. I couldn't help but admire Martin's spirit. His enthusiasm wasn't dented one bit by his failures. If anything they just made him more determined. His favourite expression was, "I'll have a Porsche before breakfast, Eddie". This passion for sports cars was matched by a passion for whisky – a potentially lethal combination, but fortunately he had a long-suffering girlfriend who was able to drive him around during his many disqualification periods. On leaving the magistrates court after one of his numerous appearances, he immediately ran over a policeman's foot.

This was the character to whom we entrusted production of our beanie bags! Our confidence was not misplaced. In all, he made 110,000 bean-bag skins for us, and I don't ever remember one of them being faulty. They were made to perfection, tiny eyes and noses all firmly inserted, leaving us to fill them with beans, and make the hats and coats. Each one was packed in its own acetate drum, and the sales were phenomenal. We must have sold well over a 100,000 of them.

Martin Downe's wedding at the Queen's Hotel Leeds, 1978.

After attending Martin's wedding to the aforementioned girlfriend at the Queen's Hotel in Leeds, we never heard from him again. I always carry a Beanie on the front dashboard of my car as a reminder of a true maverick.

One of the problems that grew in line with the Paddington craze was piracy. Counterfeit producers small and large obviously noticed our success and thought they'd like to share in it. So, fake Paddingtons started cropping up in the mid-seventies and we'd get reports of more and more of them appearing on the market. Eddie became obsessed by the problem and spent a lot of time trying to catch the pirates and put them out of business; he really did have a bee in his bonnet about them.

This wasn't just a trivial issue. Every business has to protect its name, and Gabrielle Designs was no different. It couldn't allow cheap, ugly copies – and ugly they all were – to flood the market. Our retailing clients didn't like it, and expected us to take a hard line, but more importantly the fakes could be dangerous, with eyes and noses which didn't conform to safety standards. Imagine the headlines: "Child choked to death by Paddington!" It could have put us out of business at a stroke.

WARNING

There is only one Paddington Bear

Paddington Bear is very jealous of his reputation and has become increasingly distressed by the recent manufacture of "pirate" Paddington Bears which are often ill-fed and ill-clothed. Paddington would like to inform everyone that he is produced in all three dimensional forms by

Gabrielle Designs Limited under an exclusive licence from his creator and author Michael Bond.

Gabrielle Designs Limited have also registered the design of Paddington.

During the last twelve months Michael Bond and Gabrielle Designs Limited have successfully taken legal action against the manufacturers and retailers of other fur or stuffed Bears which have either resembled the design or been colourable imitations of Paddington.

Warning is therefore given that action will continue to be taken in the future against all manufacturers and retailers of "pirate" Paddington Bears.

So please don't try to take the marmalade out of Paddington's sandwiches!

gabrielle designs Gabrielle Designs Ltd, *Home Farm, Burghwallis, Doncaster, Yorkshire.. Tel. (0302) 700516*

Paddington Bear U.K. Design Registration No. 957892 Paddington Bear U.K. Glove I Both Paddington Bear and Paddington Glove Puppet are protected by Design Registration

· BRITISH TOYS

THIS PROOF OF YOUR ADVERTISEMENT IN THE

SEPTEMBER 1975 iss

IS SENT WITH THE COMPLIMENTS OF THE ADVERTISEMENT MANAGER

Corrections should be clea marked on this proof, whi should then be returned "British Toys," Regent Hous 89 Kingsway, London WC2B 6 IMMEDIATELY, otherwise t advertisement will be printed set. Corrections may be given telephone to 01-242 9158

Chasing the pirates - the warning advertisement we placed in British toy magazines in 1975.

The problem was widespread. There were little old ladies with arthritis knitting just one bear for the church bazaar on the one hand, and on the other hand a large Jack the Lad toy manufacturer in Blackpool dressing cheap fairground bears in plastic duffle coats with boots made from oil-cloth (stuffed more than likely with old tights). We made no distinction. They all received the same stern warning from Eddie, followed by a solicitor-type letter. Sometimes the letter stopped the goings-on in their tracks; other times it had no effect at all, and a solicitor's letter followed.

Going to London one day, Eddie was telling my father about an argument he had had with a small shopkeeper in Doncaster who refused to withdraw a pirate Paddington from her window. As my father, was slightly deaf, Eddie had to speak up. On arriving at King's Cross, he stepped off the train and received an enormous right hook on the jaw. The shopkeeper's husband had been sitting behind us, and had heard every word.

Finally, Eddie reached boiling point with one unscrupulous trader from Southend-on-Sea. He had produced large numbers of a bear which wore the usual tatty duffle coat, plastic wellies, and a felt pork pie hat with a red, white, and blue ribbon round it. It was called 'Wellington'. He had ignored all warning letters, so in 1975 we took him all the way to the High Court in London. The case never actually reached the court room, because the custom at the Royal Courts of Justice is for all the parties to gather with their lawyers in a large room, coincidentally named The Bear Garden, to thrash out a settlement minutes before proceedings begin. Counsel for both sides meet in the middle of the room, argue the toss, then return to their client's corner to discuss and settle on an agreement. Then the whole thing goes before the judge, who makes the final ruling. Precedent was set that day, that if a dressed teddy bear sported two out of the three main Paddington garments, no matter what he was called, he was deemed to be a counterfeit. We were awarded compensation and costs (another expensive QC).

The press had gathered in large numbers before the hearing, not, as we thought, for us, but for the appearance in court that morning of Dorothy Squires, bringing one of her numerous actions for libel, assault, plagiarism of her autobiography, and misrepresentation, in the biography of Roger Moore, her former husband of 16 years. She looking incredibly glamorous dressed in a full-length white fur coat and hat, but she didn't attract as much attention as Paddington, standing in the middle of The Bear Garden. The photographers crowded around us, I was taken out to stand in front of those familiar railings of the RCJ, and photographed with hundreds of silly expressions on my face, whilst poor Dorothy slipped away unnoticed.

The newspapers next morning all carried banner headlines proclaiming "Victory for a little bear!" Their reporters had gone to town with puns on the word bear, so we had "company bearing up", "grin and bear it", "the bear facts", "bear faced cheek", "bearable", to name but a few. They were all pretty gruesome, but I can hardly talk – look at the title of this book!

Copy cats crushed

PADDINGTON Bear took his imitators to court yesterday and ended up victorious.

Bobby the Dog retired defeated and Jubilee Bear walked off barefoot, having been stripped of his Wellingtons.

The scene of the confrontation was the aptly-named Bear Garden at London's High Court, where a judge sits in private to hear disputes.

Paddington, dressed smartly in red duffle coat, shiny red boots and blue floppy hat, was accompanied by his designer, Mrs Shirley Clarkson, pictured, and her husband Edward, whose company — Gabrielle Designs of Doncaster — sought an order against a rival firm.

K W Clarke (Foam) of Southend was responsible for marketing Bobby the Dog, Jubilee Bear and other similarly dressed bears.

K W Clarke agreed to withdraw Bobby the Dog and all dogs and bears dressed similarly to Paddington from the market. It agreed to take off Jubilee Bear's red Wellingtons and put him back on sale barefoot. And it also agreed to pay Gabrielle Designs damages and legal costs.

Me after our victory at the High Court in 1975.

On the home front, there were one or two episodes. Jeremy's headmaster at Repton, a patient gentleman, had finally had enough of his antics, and politely suggested that he return home, and re-visit the school only to sit his A-levels. Jeremy had been threatened with expulsion before – something to do with an explosion in the science block – but had told the headmaster on that occasion that the shock would prove fatal for his father, who "had a weak heart". His silver tongue bought him time, even if what he said was nonsense: Eddie had health problems galore, but his heart was never one of them.

1978 was a turning point, when things started to go wrong for Gabrielle. We made the mistake (again) of thinking that we needed an office manager. We followed all the right procedures this time, advertising it everywhere, from *Caravan Monthly* to *The Budgerigar Times*. Happy to say, we found the ideal candidate, a lovely man called Bill, who I had acted with in the Thespians all those years ago, and whose wonderful sense of humour, acting ability and beautiful singing I had never forgotten. He had made a superb Jack Point in *The Yeomen of the Guard*, but, as were to discover, this is not necessarily the right basis on which to appoint an office manager.

Bill kept the office spotless, and bought lots of pretty ringbinders, notebooks, and files in which to keep lists of things. We bought him a dinky little car, in brown, which squeaked every morning as it crept slowly down the drive. He wanted a sign painted on the wall of the yard, 'Reserved for W. J. Owen', but as he was the only employee with a car, it seemed a bit ridiculous. Immaculately dressed, he carried a briefcase in which he brought his apple for lunch and 20 cigarettes for after lunch! Alas, he was useless.

Instead of taking pressure off Eddie and me, Bill's presence merely added to it. Eddie, in particular, felt the stress. One day in February he came home complaining of feeling unwell, went straight to bed, and stayed there for a year. Quoting Hilaire Belloc:

Physicians of the utmost fame

Were called at once

But when they came

They answered as they took their fees

There is no cure for this disease

Eddie's symptoms followed no particular pattern. He had acute back pain, but scans and X-rays revealed no cause. A couple of years previously he had foolishly tried to lift our caravan whilst its legs were still down, and had damaged a vertebra in his neck, but that had healed. Looking back now, I realise that it was just the enormous pressure of the business that had taken its toll on him.

Eddie's absence came at the worst possible time. We were reaching the peak of Paddington sales, with 87,000 bears sold in 1978, over 11,000 of them in November. The order books had been closed since January that year, and we devised an alphabetical system of despatching, which meant that if you were Abacus you got your delivery on the 1st of the month whilst retailers at the bottom end of the alphabet, like poor old Walrus & Carpenter, were lucky to get theirs by the 31st.

Bill was busy dusting, Betty was miffed at Bill's dusting and handed in her notice (I didn't think much of her timing), Eddie was laid up in bed suffering, Jeremy was wreaking havoc at Repton, and Joanna was home from school with her third bout of ME, sitting in a chair staring into space, hardly having the energy to breathe. Don't ever let anyone tell you that ME is all in the mind. It's real, it's debilitating, and it's frightening.

To top it all, the factory inspector was threatening to close us down because the magnetic catches on our stuffing machine didn't conform to Health and Safety specifications.

With the business already creaking under the strain, I, in my wisdom, decided it was the right time to introduce a new product – a Paddington suitcase. Inside the suitcase, there was to be a marmalade sandwich, a sepia photograph of Aunt Lucy, and a Peruvian coin called a *sol*, which was legal tender in Peru at that time. The sandwich was no problem – simply two sheets of white polystyrene foam, with a sheet of orange felt stuck between, punched out by a triangular cutter (with a bite out). The photograph was easy too, just a simple print job with the photo inserted into a tiny cardboard frame. The genuine Peruvian sol proved a little more difficult.

I was adamant that the sol had to be the real thing, and after fruitless conversations with the Peruvian Embassy and the Bank of Lima in London, my father, then in his late seventies, offered to fly over and collect some from Peru. Known affectionately to everyone as 'Bumper' by this time, he was convinced he could persuade the manager to hand over the hard currency, and he loved a challenge. He had just been diagnosed with angina, but made the doctor swear that he would not divulge this to anyone, and as his aorta was not in too good a nick, it was agreed that my sister Pat would accompany him.

We booked them on a flight to Miami, where they had a trip to Disneyland, and Bumper bought himself a Mickey Mouse t-shirt, then they caught a flight to Lima. Apparently the smog never lifts from the Peruvian capital. It is permanently grey and dismal, desperately unattractive, and poor to a horrific degree. My father suggested a trip up to Lake Titicaca, high in the Andes. At that altitude, he would undoubtedly have made the return trip in a body bag, but Pat persuaded him that it was not a good idea, and instead he set off for the Bank Nationale in downtown Lima wearing his Mickey Mouse t-shirt from Disneyland and smoking through a long cigarette holder.

Now, I said earlier that my father liked a challenge, but he didn't speak a word of Spanish, the bank manager was equally bereft of English, and the prospects of a successful meeting must have been slim. Nevertheless, Bumper began his pitch. He related how his daughter Shirley back in England made bears called Paddington "like the railway station", who incidentally came from Lima. "In fact, his Aunt Lucy still resides here in a home for retired bears and his Uncle Pastuso distils cocoa up in the mountains of Darkest Peru." He went on to describe how Paddington carried a suitcase in which there was a sol, and then asked the critical question: please could he have some?

Somehow the bank manager got the gist of what he was saying – the last bit, anyway – and to my father's astonishment, he actually agreed to his request. Bumper left the bank with a large sackful of sol, each worth half a farthing. History does not record whether the bank manager ever really comprehended why this strange, deaf, seventy year-old Englishman had flown halfway around the world to ask for some sol. Perhaps he handed them over just to get Bumper off the premises.

The mission was accomplished, but not before another near-disaster. The poverty in Lima was so acute at that time that locals had removed all the iron manhole covers to sell for scrap. That fact, coupled with Bumper's fascination for birds, resulted in an almost cartoon-like mishap. As he walked along the street, gazing at the birds perched high on the rooftops (my sister swears they could only have been vultures), he fell straight down a manhole, still clutching his sack of sol, and had to be dragged out ignominiously, a little dazed but fortunately unscathed.

He and Pat arrived back at Heathrow without further incident, causing mayhem at customs, but never mind – Paddington had real sol in his suitcase!

Unfortunately, it all had been to no avail. The suitcases had been beautifully designed and made, with a gold embossed 'PB' on the lid, a secret compartment, and a 'Wanted on Voyage' label, but they had no check straps which meant that the lid could be forced right back, dislodging the hinges from the body of the case. Customers were returning them to us slightly faster than we were sending them out. In our usual optimistic way, we had ordered thousands of the little cases, so we couldn't just adjust the design. We had to withdraw all the ones we'd already sent out, and put them on a bonfire with our unsold stock. Only the sol were spared.

That was a minor hitch compared to the one that followed. In February 1979, we took delivery of 50,000 pairs of plastic eyes, complete with metal washers, from a supplier in London who we had used from the earliest days of Gabrielle Designs. These eyes and washers were inserted in bears, and shipped to virtually every corner of the globe. It was not until July that the first hint of trouble manifested itself. One or two bears were returned, with complaints that the eyes had either become glazed or had fallen out. The one-offs turned into a small trickle, with distraught children (and adults) sending tear-stained letters begging us to mend and return their bear, and it had to be their bear, it was no good sending a new one. The trickle became a flood: hundreds of bears, lorry loads in some cases, arrived back at our factory, until piles of the sightless little chaps littered the floor, and this all happened in late summer when Christmas production was in full swing.

Remedying this problem was a monumental task. Each bear had to be slit down the back of his head, unstuffed down to his neck, the eyes replaced, and then re-stuffed and sewn up. Eddie was beginning to undertake a little work again, and helped pack 'recuperating' bears into boxes, with a marmalade sandwich, a bandage round his head, a letter saying what a good patient he had been, and a red cross on the lid. But mending the bears was only the half of it. We also had to make sure that each bear was returned to his rightful owner. It was no good sending Johnny's bear to Jane and vice versa. The documentation was unbelievable!

13th June,,1979

Dear Customer,

U R G E N T

Unfortunately we are experiencing certain problems with Paddington's eyes used since February/March 1979. The eyes in the large bears are safety eyes held with a metal washer gripping the shank at the back. For reasons which are being investigated with the greatest diligence,some eyes are becoming glazed, giving Paddington a 'blind look'. The black pupil is completely eliminated, leaving a plain orange eye ball, resulting in the eye eventually breaking off. (If the black pupil has, in certain lights, 6 slight light marks around the edge in symetrical pattern, this is normal and is only Paddington's 'starry' look).
We should be most grateful if you would examine your stock and return to us any bears which have this defect and we shall of course, replace the eyes and return, refunding all carriage charges.
We do apologise most sincerely for this inconvenience but we feel it is better to check all bears before they reach the hands of adoring owners, and Paddington's reputation for remarkable quality is blemished.

Yours very sincerely
GABRIELLE DESIGNS LIMITED

Shirley Clarkson.

Shirley G. Clarkson.

Our letter to customers about Paddington's faulty eyes, 1979.

To cap it all, we couldn't just repair the bears that were returned to us. We also had to warn other customers, whose bears might have been perfectly alright, that they *might* have a problem, which we did by taking out advertisements and sending out letters. Our biggest fear was that a child would swallow an eye and choke. Thankfully that did not happen, and no one suffered any injury, but the whole episode was immensely draining and expensive. One customer, a Mrs Coote (we always remembered her name, because we considered her as daft as one) lived in New Zealand, and her bear suffered the dreaded eye complaint. She thought it was because she'd left him on the car window shelf in the sun, so we never let on. However, distraught, she booked two seats (one for her, the other for Paddington!) first class, on a Qantas plane, took a taxi from Heathrow to The Bear Garden (150 miles), and wanted the bear to have an operation, done privately obviously. She was in such a nervous state, I had to take her out for lunch, and convince her that Paddy would have an anaesthetic and would feel no pain at all. Thelma in her usual brusque Yorkshire way, said, "Didn't you tell 'er we slit 'is 'ead open, smash 'is eyes on the concrete t'floor and 'ammer new eyes in?" No, I didn't. Alas, she wasn't happy: she said he didn't have the same look as before!

Thelma, as usual, came up trumps during this crisis, managing to keep production going at the same time as running an ophthalmic surgical ward. That left me free to concentrate on the litigation side of the problem. Obviously *somebody had to pay* for the mistake. We ascertained that our eye supplier, Mrs M., as I shall call her (although we used other names for her as the months progressed), had used cheaper, inferior plastic to make the eyes. At the same time, she had changed her supplier of metal washers, and the new ones she used had smaller holes than the old ones – only fractions of a millimetre smaller, but the result was that the washer gripped the shank of the eye too tightly, and after about six months the plastic could no longer stand the strain and cracked, thus causing the eyeball to fall out, leaving the shank inside the bear. Mrs M. hotly denied responsibility, but agreed to visit The Bear Garden to see the problem for herself.

Coventry
October '22-

Dear Mrs. Clarkson,

Thank you very much for returning Paddington. He looks really super again.

He stands on my high bookcase where my dog Sika can not reach him. The day he attacked Paddington he took him off my dressing table. We found Paddingtons red wellingtons on my bed his hat on the floor and Paddington under the bed.

I spent ages looking at the Paddingtons in the shop - who all looked very new so I could mend my bear but I could not have hoped he would

look as good as he does again. I was very upset and cross with Sika the night it happened as Paddington is one of the nicest presents I have had.

Everyone thinks he is nice and would like to have one. They are all nice it took me ages to choose one, your factory must look lovely with Paddingtons everywhere.

Thank you very much for all your time and trouble, it was very kind of everybody as you all must be busy making new Paddingtons.

Yours sincerely, Andrea ▓▓▓

A letter from a young Paddington owner whose Bear we mended, 1978.

By the time the fault surfaced, we had despatched about 35,000 dodgy-eyed bears, and had a further 15,000 in stock, ready for the Christmas rush. On her visit, Mrs M. was asked to pick any box at random, and we would empty it out in her presence. From every box she picked, about six out of the fifteen eyes were faulty, so she silently slipped on her full-length suede coat, got into her chauffeur-driven Daimler, and sped back to Soho.

There followed some hilarious trips by myself and our solicitor to Imperial College in London, where they have a top-notch metallurgy department. We had to prove that the metal in the new washers differed from the old, and we did this by dropping them on to a marble table. One washer went "ping" whilst the other went "pung". Very scientific. We had to sit blindfolded whilst the professor dropped the washers, and we had to say "ping" or "pung". It seemed to work, as we could accurately tell pings from pungs, but it was all to no avail because Mrs M., seeing the writing on the wall, put her company into voluntary liquidation before we could issue a writ. The upshot was that we simply had to destroy all the eyes and washers, lick our wounds, and carry on. I seem to remember assessing the damage at around £40,000, but never had the time or inclination to sit down and work it out. Because a month later, in January 1979, my darling Bumper died of an aneurysm. We were setting up a photo shoot for *The Sunday Times*, when Father's partner rang to say he had collapsed and was on his way to hospital. I regret to this day that the photographer persuaded me to remain long enough for him to get a shot or two. Those few minutes deprived me of seeing Bumper before he lost consciousness. I arrived at the hospital just too late.

I remember the horror of entering the church for the funeral service, and a tactless old bugger congratulating us. Apparently, it had been announced in *The Times* that morning that Gabrielle Designs had turned over £1,000,000.

Chapter Nine – Our Graham

When things can't get any worse, create something, that's my way of dealing with things. I don't think it's a method recommended by business schools, but it works for me.

At the start of 1979, we were beset by problems both business and personal: Eddie's health was not good, the faulty eye episode had cost us dear, Bill was a square peg in a round hole, and we'd wasted money on Paddington suitcases. All that, coupled with the death of Bumper, and it was shaping up as an *annus horribilis*.

My response was to work flat-out on a new product: Aunt Lucy. One of the reasons I chose her was that we always insisted that any Paddington character we made should be completely faithful to Michael's books, and we had exhausted the possibilities with Paddington himself. I was constantly being asked to design him wearing a Caribbean shirt, a Santa Clause outfit, an Elvis Presley jacket, even a Manchester United strip. No, he wore a duffle coat, hat, and wellies, and that was that.

Aunty Lucy offered us new scope. In the books, she had come over from Peru to watch a rugby match between the Peruvian Reserves and the Portobello Wanderers. Somehow or other Paddington received an invitation to the match, and of course he ended up on the pitch, scoring the winning try.

Aunt Lucy was a designer's dream. She wore all the genuine Peruvian gear: black bowler hat, striped shawl, little felt slippers, and gold-rimmed spectacles on a chain around her neck. The shawl was easy. Doncaster market was renowned for its numerous fabric stalls, remnants from the defunct woollen mills in Bradford, and Leeds no doubt. I found endless bolts of brightly-coloured striped cloth, suitable for her shawl. Her fur had to be changed to an aging grey, which presented no problem, but it meant we received more visits from the Bury Masco area representative, a man who would today be described in politically correct terms as "follicly challenged". He sported a wig which I swear was made from a remnant of PB fur – you could even see the woven backing – wore apple green nylon shirts, and on hot days, after a long journey, insisted that you run your hand up his back to feel how much he was sweating! Take note, any budding sales representatives, that is *not* how to impress your customer, and swell your order book.

The bowler hat proved a little more difficult. We had to pay a hat manufacturer several thousand pounds to construct a hat-making mould. In shoe circles, it's called a last, but I've no idea what the equivalent is in the world of millinery. Once we had the mould, we got the long-suffering and ever-obliging Bury Masco to make the thick black felt. My attention to detail was such that I even had the hatband specially woven from a design I found in a Peruvian travel brochure.

The clever bit was Aunt Lucy's bloomers! Ankle length in red flannel, or crisp white calico, with a pocket containing a sol, reclaimed from the suitcase disaster. Every cloud, etc. etc.

Special edition Aunt Lucy.

Obviously, Aunt Lucy didn't sell as well as her illustrious nephew, but she did okay. By the time she was launched, Eddie was making a brave attempt to get back to work. While he'd been away, I had kept the administrative side of the company more or less in order with the help of a very good team, but it wasn't my forte and my methods were fairly primitive. Some companies in the late seventies may have been using computers, but we still relied on pen and paper, and walls of lever arch files. Eddie was obviously concerned as to what I was doing, and his return was much needed. He came into the office one morning, and before I could start to tell him the state of the business, he had removed all my books and papers, put them in a neat pile on the floor, and seated himself at his desk as if he'd never been away.

Whether he could no longer bear to look at my paperwork, or he was just itching to see customers, it wasn't long before he set out on the road again. His customers were always thrilled to see him, but alas I received phone calls from many of them, saying that Eddie had called, and they were extremely worried about him. He was obviously not fit to be driving, he was still in great pain, his asthma had deteriorated into emphysema and pseudomonas, a debilitating lung complaint, and sometimes the only relief was alcohol. I tried to persuade Eddie to take it easy, to spend less time on the road, but he loved it so much, and was so stubborn that my entreaties fell on deaf ears.

Joanna, meanwhile, was still recovering from her bout of ME. She had struggled back to Malvern after nine months at home (thank goodness for education insurance!) and was trying to catch up with her lost education.

Alarmingly, there were rumblings of discontent at the office too. Bill, I fear had been asked to leave; Betty had got fed up with Bill and already left; Thelma, meanwhile, was turning into a megalomaniac. She now hated me with a passion, resented me coming anywhere near the factory, and finally walked out in a fit of temper. Being a brilliant manager, she considered the factory her domain and hers alone, so if I arrived with the plans for my latest design to be put into production, she felt I was deliberately trying to disrupt her routine. I usually received a sharp "Bugger off!" which I could stand to a point, but one morning, probably with a severe dose of PMT, I flipped and told her to be quiet. Off she went, across the fields, leaving the company van which she normally drove behind her, and we never saw her again.

Having been evicted by Eddie from the office, Thelma's departure at least meant I had somewhere to go. I took up the reins at the factory again.

Time to make another dramatic blunder – appoint another manager! This time there would be no mistake. The advertisements were inserted everywhere, and out of eighty-eight applicants (isn't it strange how you remember certain facts, but can never remember where you last put your specs?) we shortlisted twenty-two, the crème de la crème, so to speak.

For some unearthly reason we decided to hold the interviews at a motel miles away from Doncaster. For three days Eddie and I sat in a dreary conference room in Selby, drinking filthy coffee, listening to witless idiots babbling on about how brilliant they were. It probably wasn't much fun for the candidates, but it was hell for us.

After the first ten or so had filed in and out again, we completely lost track of which questions we'd asked and kept on repeating ourselves. It was obvious as some of them came round the door that they were totally unfit for the job, but to be fair to them we had to give them their allotted time and go through the motions. I know how Simon Cowell feels! I remember one particularly unimpressive specimen who had cycled four or five miles, and when asked if he had any expenses said that a couple of quid would come in handy!

Then, hallelujah! in walked Graham!

So that you can understand how impressive Graham was, let me give you some background on Eddie's likes and dislikes. If there was one thing he couldn't abide it was a man with a beard. Facial hair was unacceptable in whatever shape or form. He also strongly disapproved of obesity, and he hated plastic shoes. Any hint of any of these three was enough to disbar a candidate from the job, but they were nothing compared to the importance of a man's handshake. Eddie had a fundamentalist view on the matter: a handshake was a window on a man's soul and if it was anything less than a vice-like grip, the individual must have serious character weaknesses.

So, in walked Graham. He weighed around twenty-four stone, had a naval beard, his orange shoes were reconstituted vinyl, and his handshake reminded you of a haddock.

And then began an amazing transformation. Slowly, Graham overturned all our prejudices and convinced us that he was the person we were looking for. He impressed us with his knowledge of Paddington, even to the point of having read up on the origins of the duffle coat. He skilfully mentioned his time at Southampton University (later revealed to have been a three week computer course). He regaled us with stories of how he had built his own cooker and made his own printed circuits for the television to save costs. We were captivated. Graham was brilliant, obviously the man for us! We made him a job offer on the spot, and he accepted immediately.

Within a week, Graham had taken up his post at The Bear Garden, where his enthusiasm and geniality charmed the girls, even if his girth didn't. His one stipulation was that Eddie and I kept our distance. He wanted complete control, he said. We had to trust him to do the job without interference. Fair enough, we thought. A dynamic individual like Graham needs freedom in which to exercise his talents.

He also needed a computer to modernise our stone-age systems, and we were happy to oblige his request (though, given his boasts at interview, we should have wondered why he didn't build his own).

The arrangement was that Graham would come down to Home Farm every Monday morning and give us a report on the previous week's output, sales, stock levels, costing updates, and staff performances, etc. This seemed very sensible, and to start with all went well. The inches-thick pile of computer printouts he lugged in every week was so daunting we really thought that he must be doing a fantastic job. He talked sense, and brimmed with confidence. There were no panic signals from the rest of the staff. Eddie and I congratulated ourselves on *finally* – third time lucky – appointing the manager we had always needed.

Our problem was that we desperately *wanted* him to be doing a fantastic job, because we needed to rid ourselves of the stress of running the business. Sales were jogging along nicely, and with Graham's hand on the tiller, I could spend more time designing, sourcing fabrics and generally keeping an eye on production, making sure that standards were maintained. That was the theory, anyway.

Chapter Ten – Sailing into Troubled Waters

With Graham in charge of all the boring administrative tasks at Gabrielle, I was free to concentrate on new creative ideas, and I didn't waste any time. One of the opportunities that arose in 1979 was to design and manufacture soft toys based on the 'Captain Beaky and His Band' books written by Jeremy Lloyd and illustrated by the renowned Shakespearean actor, Keith Michell. Keith's superb drawings complemented Jeremy's stories perfectly and the books went on to become deserved bestsellers in the eighties.

The idea of creating toys to go with the books appealed to me enormously. The book's six main characters – Captain Beaky, a cross between a chicken and a duck, Reckless Rat, Artful Owl, Timid Toad, Batty Bat, and Hissing Sid, the snake – were wonderfully vivid, oozed potential, and I couldn't wait to get started. We went down to London (Yorkshire folk refuse to say "Up to London") and met Keith and Jeremy together with Jim Parker, the musician who had composed the songs. I would have been happy to have just got a kiss from Keith and gone home – he was SO charming – but we got down to business quite quickly and began discussing what the character toys might look like. Now I consider myself a perfectionist in these matters, but compared to Keith, I'm a sloppy "couldn't-give-a-damn" sort of gal. At the very first meeting we were talking about fine details like the positioning of Beaky's eyes, the shading on the underside of Bat's wings, and the method we were going to use to spray Hissing Sid's skin, totally ignoring the question of whether or not there would be a market for the toys, who would be likely to buy them, the price, and other such vital issues which designers don't consider very important.

Captain Beaky and His Band, 1979.

Back at HQ, Graham was ensconced in the factory, counting ears and toggles, and putting all the stock onto his computer database. He was obsessed about making machines that would help to speed up production and installed an enormous revolving wire brush to brush

153

out the seams on Paddington. On its test run, he approached it with a bear, but the brush was so powerful that it whipped the head clean off, propelling it across the room. Another invention was a machine which weighed the correct amount of pellets with which to fill the bean bags. It usually sent the pellets flying everywhere, and was more trouble than it was worth – using a plastic tooth mug and a kitchen funnel had worked well for years. But he was obviously happy and it left me free to set up a little design room in the local post office which Gabrielle had purchased after buying all the barns in the neighbourhood. It was cosy, if a bit spartan, with a coal fire, and a little kitchen for making endless coffees. Kristina and I were joined by June, a quite remarkable lady, with enormous flair, and a sense of humour to match. We three sat around the fire, creating quite ludicrous designs of the Beaky Band. Captain Beaky was made in white felt, with real feathers hand stitched around his body, and wire-framed legs covered in yellow felt, and sported a naval captain's hat, correct in every detail. The felt bodies of the owl and snake were sprayed through stencils with what I'm quite sure was toxic paint. Any concerns we had about toy safety were overcome by attaching labels to the products stating that they were not toys, but collectibles! We'd never get away with that today.

Reckless Rat was fabulous. He was made in top grade suede, with a greatcoat in blue leather. For some reason Keith wanted him in a cowboy's hat, which proved no problem for our hat manufacturer. "So you now want cowboy hats for rats do you?" Well, they were easier than bowlers for bears.

Batty Bat was in grey and pink suede with incredibly intricate embroidery under his wings.

I can't remember how many trips we made to London for meetings with Keith, but each one became more frustrating than the last. He is an artist, and a brilliant one, but he had no inkling how difficult it was for us to transpose his drawings into three dimensional saleable items. He would spend hours bending and twisting the feathers to get them to his liking. Did he not realise that they were going to be shoved in a box, transported by a carrier, probably upside down, and piled up in Hamleys storeroom for weeks, then put on display in the shop, knocked on the floor, and kicked up and down the aisles along with a platoon of Action Men? It would be amazing if they had any feathers left on them at all, after that.

Despite all the tribulations, we eventually settled on designs for the six characters and in early 1980 the factory started making them alongside Paddington. Six weeks later they were on the shelves of toyshops up and down the country. That is the great advantage of having a track record in an industry – you can follow up your winner (in our case Paddington) with other products and the trade will give you the benefit of the doubt, which they would never do for a complete newcomer.

My misgivings about some of the over-fussy designs in the Captain Beaky range were born out when Joanna had a holiday job in the Harrods toy department the following year. I remember creeping up behind her as she worked on the till and watching as a very smart gentleman (obviously naval) selected a Captain Beaky and placed it on the counter. To my horror, I noticed that Beaky's body had slithered down over his legs, wrinkling the yellow felt till they looked like Nora Batty's stockings. His feathers had definitely not withstood the journey, and he had been fingered by far too many customers.

As Joanna saw this tatty object placed before her she enquired "Do you really want this, Sir? It's very dirty, and do you realise it's £29.95?" Thank goodness she went into law, and not sales! Actually the only reason she opted for the law was because after a year at Lucy Clayton's School for Young Ladies (where you learn how to alight from a Ferrari without showing your knickers), she had a lecture from a very handsome barrister, and was inspired to follow him into the profession. Little did she realize that most lawyers look more like Rumpole than George Clooney.

We eventually managed to get all the Beaky gang on the market, although I doubt whether the royalties from them made Keith very rich. Who cares, we had had a wonderful time in the post office, lots of kisses from Keith, and we were secure in the knowledge that Graham had the business under control.

Oh dear, had we but known.

Eddie and I had been running Gabrielle Designs for over 15 years now, mostly at full speed, and we'd got to that stage where we wanted to enjoy the fruits of our labours. One cold wet miserable day in February 1980, he read in the *Yorkshire Post* about a company based in Leeds which was offering shares in a motor cruiser called 'Sizzler', to be moored in the South of France. The deal was, you got a fortnight per annum for ten years, for £5,000. To view Sizzler we had to travel twenty miles to Wakefield, where we found her bobbing about on a lake in the sleet. We were greeted by three charming, well-presented men – red braces, Porsches, the works. Not a beard between them, their handshakes were firm, and their shoes leather. Within minutes we were signed up. I mean the boat was magnificent! Dralon sofas, tasselled light shades, plastic gladioli, white simulated leather sun loungers, and best of all, a little hatch from the kitchen to the driver's seat, just large enough to pass a Pimms through – what more could you want? Well it did have two engines underneath somewhere.

We thought we would take two fortnights because Jeremy wouldn't want to come with us. We'd let him take a bunch of responsible 20 year-old mates from Repton for two weeks, and we would take Joanna, and her incredibly gorgeous, albeit lazy, school friend Jillie for the other two.

So, the deal struck was four weeks a year, for ten years, for £10,000.

One small snag. To enable us to move Sizzler out from La Napoule harbour, where she would be moored, we had to have a Master Mariner's certificate. Eddie wasn't too keen on doing the necessary training, so the children and I signed up for a week's instruction with a very dodgy retired sea captain. His boat resembled an up-ended cornflake packet floating on Southampton Water, but he said that he had spectacular success rates with his students and for a large fee was willing to take us on the Solent and instruct us in the very simple art of boating. Apparently, today this training involves years of intensive study, almost to degree standard, but he said he could teach us everything we needed to know in a week.

Jeremy did his week first in a one-to-one session with the Captain and passed with flying colours. Joanna and I followed the week after. As we pulled out of the harbour Joanna turned the colour of mushy peas. It was choppy, and this vessel's stabilisers were not exactly state-of-the-art. Eventually we made it to Cowes, and there, watched by a group of sailing diehards, we took it in turns to master the art of reversing into tight spaces without removing too much paint from adjoining boats. I can't remember the captain's name, but he had a long beard and drank heavily. We learned to navigate using a hand-held compass, draw compass roses and, using a sweeping brush handle and the draining board, plot courses. We did sheep shanks, and bowlines, and reef knots; we wound up ropes and generally had a bloody good time.

It helped that Captain was a brilliant cook, and produced wonderful dinners, but on about the third day, he went ashore for several hours, and returned with an Australian lady. From then on he spent most of his day and night locked in his cabin, presumably singing Sea Shanties with his new friend!

Towards the end of the week Captain announced that we would have to sit an exam to enable him to award us our certificates. Now Joanna had always taken her studies very seriously, she didn't do "failing", and was in a state of nervous frenzy at the thought of this forthcoming test. To put us at ease, Captain suggested that we should try one of last year's papers, and get the gist of what was required. It was unbelievable: the questions made not a word of sense: "How often should you grease your nipples?" "Do you wind your ropes clockwise or anticlockwise?" What the hell were wind vectors?

We handed in the papers feeling very down-in-the-mouth. Justifiably so. I got 11% and Joanna 13%. It seemed like our dreams of sailing the Med were dashed. Captain was strangely upbeat, considering the manifest incompetence of his students. He tried to restore our spirits, going through each of the questions with us and explaining where we had gone wrong. He said he was confident that we could improve enough in the real exam to pass.

We didn't sleep a wink that night, partly out of worry, and partly because of the bonking in the adjoining cabin. Morning came and we sat down for the big exam. Out of the customary brown envelope Captain pulled the papers with great solemnity, and then, with a gentle smile, handed us exactly the same questions as we had seen the day before. We aced it. Joanna got 97% and I got 96%. We later discovered that Jeremy had benefited from similar generosity on Captain's part, but never let on to me and Joanna, having been sworn to secrecy. No wonder Captain's pass rates were so good.

There we were, qualified sailors, ready to take on whatever the Med might throw at us, but without so much as a thimbleful of maritime expertise between us. Terrifying! Unfortunately, the driver of the low-loader carrying Sizzler down the M1 to the ferry jammed on his brakes rather too violently at the end of the motorway, and Sizzler shot forward, landing on her nose in the fast lane. We were assured that the damage was only minor, and eventually she was moored up at La Napoule, in a magnificent harbour under the care of a gorgeous Dutchman called Bart. We loaded up, filling the fridge with langouste, pâté, and melons, and stocking the shelves with wine and Pimms, the essential M&S fruit cake, and tea bags. The girls crammed numerous bottles of shampoo, conditioner and gel into the shower/loo (fully flushing!) and off we sailed, me at the helm, Joanna carelessly tossing the ropes on to the quayside, and all of us giving Bart a cheery wave.

We had a map, and decided to head east, or was it west? Towards St. Tropez, anyway. Jo stood on the pointed bit, and stuck her arm out to alert any following ships that we were turning that way! Boats don't have indicators. Eddie was his usual sartorial self, no sloppy deck shoes for him. He polished his brown lace-ups every morning, and sported a naval blazer and tie, and grey flannels with knife edge creases. He was content to let me do nearly all the steering while Jo and Jillie took charge of the anchor!

On the first night we were due to moor at San Raphael, a task that was made considerably more difficult by the gale that was blowing and the rocks that guarded the entrance to the harbour. Joanna and I scrutinized the buoys that were meant to guide us in, but could not remember what the colours and shapes meant. "Western Women Want Waspie Waists" meant, we were sure, that if there were two triangles on top of the buoy you had to keep to the west of it, or was it that you *mustn't* keep to the west of it? Oh dear. If only we had listened to Captain more attentively.

We had no choice but to guess and hope for the best. We must have struck lucky, because we made it to the relative shelter inside the harbour wall. Relief washed over us – temporarily. There was still the mooring and tying up to do. In the Med you have to reverse into parking spaces. If you get it just slightly wrong, the wind catches your nose end, you are propelled down the wall side, and an angry Capitaine shouts at you a lot. If you have been allocated mooring 286, and you skid down to 294, he's not pleased. The terror of trying to perform this manoeuvre in front of a crowd of contemptuous Frenchmen still gives me the shudders. After several failed attempts, we finally made it into our slot, to a round of sarcastic applause from the dockside.

The Harbour Master then shouted at us, demanding a "poulet". Now we definitely didn't have a chicken on board, but apparently *poulie* is French for pulley. We definitely didn't have a pulley either. After a great deal more shouting in French he switched to English, which would have helped in the beginning.

"From where 'ave you come?" he enquired.

"La Napoule," we replied.

"And 'ow were you tied up in La Napoule?"

"With ropes."

"And where are ze ropes now?"

"Er … on the quay in La Napoule."

He reluctantly threw us a rope, and I sent Joanna over the side to attach the boat to the metal ring in the wall. With tears of laughter rolling down her face, she popped up and said "Mother, does the little rabbit go round the tree twice before going down the hole?"

Amazing how quickly you learn though. From that unpromising start, we got better and better and by the time we reached St. Tropez we could navigate, park, tie up and boil a kettle all at the same time.

Unlike some sailors, we kept our perspective: we didn't spend our evenings polishing our cleats or swabbing decks, but showered, changed into little casual numbers, and headed off into town for dinner. Those little bistros in the back streets of Antibes, St Jeanne, and Lavandou were fabulous, and the peaceful bays around Cap Ferrat and Cap D'Antibes, where you could drop anchor at lunchtime, get legless on Pimms, stuff yourself with prawns, snooze in the sun, and swim in the warm clear blue waters before heading for the next marina of your choice were delights that will live with me till I die. No holiday I've ever had – before or since – will come anywhere close to those weeks on Sizzler.

Monte Carlo was on the itinerary, but was definitely not our favourite place on the Riviera. You have a choice there of the quaint old harbour or the glitzy new one, open to the east. We fancied hobnobbing with the rich and famous, so aimed for the glitzy one. A blazing row with the harbour master followed. He considered Sizzler to be far too puny a boat to be allowed to rub hulls with the 100-metre behemoths already moored there, and refused to let us in. "Complét!" seems to be a favourite word used against English sailors, but the girls going topless always helped to get us in.

It was as we were manoeuvring towards the quay – which is not so much a solid wall as a shelf in Monte Carlo – that Eddie's talent for injuring himself was once again on display. In an effort to steady Sizzler, he jumped onto the bathing platform at the back of the boat ready to push with his hands against the shelf if we came too close. Unfortunately, there was a hell of a storm brewing up out to sea at the time, and this was creating a lot of swell in the harbour. Sizzler was heaving up and down, and in one of the down lurches she was swept under the shelf, coming up with great force. It's a miracle that Eddie wasn't sliced in two.

Because of the storm, we were unable to leave harbour, and were forced to endure Monte Carlo for three days, a fate I would not wish on my worst enemy. It isn't glamorous; it's ugly, vulgar and infested by tax-dodgers and chancers. Not my idea of fun. Our irritation was made worse by the fact that, without the engine running, we didn't have hot water, and were unable to wash. Eddie insisted that we leave port, head west again, and put in to the old harbour which was sheltered from the east wind. The rest of us were right behind him so, as inconspicuously as we could, we dropped anchor and headed for the open sea.

We didn't even get as far as the harbour exit before we were spotted. We watched the faces of hardened sailors on the quayside, aghast at our recklessness. No fool would be daft enough to go out in a Force 7, would they? Well, we had washing to do, and nothing comes between an Englishman and his smalls. Besides, we fancied a look at Cannes.

As we approached the harbour gate, we saw an enormous tanker disappear from view as it went into the trough of a wave three times its height, and you didn't have to be Chay Blyth to realize that these were not the conditions little Sizzler was built for. Common sense prevailed over bulldog bravado, and we spent an hour or so circling the buoy in the middle of Monte Carlo harbour, with a line full of knickers fluttering in the wind. I bet they are still talking about those "English fools" in the Palace to this day.

We had two more idyllic holidays on Sizzler, but unfortunately two days before we were due to leave for the third one, Eddie decided to fall and break his hip. Had I been a good wife, I would have cancelled the trip and sat by his bedside, making soothing noises, but Joanna and Jillie had already set off by car to cross France, and were due to meet us at La Napoule. There were no mobile phones in those days, and we had no idea where they were, so I convinced myself without much difficulty that I should go without Eddie, and not disappoint them. My sister joined us, and we spent a week astounding the Mediterranean boat people with our total ineptitude.

The following year, everything went pear-shaped with the three gentlemen from Leeds. For their business to be viable, they needed to sell timeshares to at least ten people, but they had only managed to sign up five. Their palatial offices in Leeds, and their endless all-expenses trips abroad, ostensibly to attract customers, had drained them of cash so that they were unable to pay either the boatyard, maintenance costs, or the French equivalent of VAT. They came to see us on the eve of our departure in year four, arriving in a Ford Fiesta, and said that although we could go, there would not be any maintenance carried out on the boat, and the usual starter pack of Champagne in the fridge might be missing. They weren't kidding. Only one of the Volvo engines was working, the boat was filthy, and Bart seemed to play "Hidey" whenever we needed him.

Shortly afterwards, the whole company collapsed, we lost the rest of our money, and Sizzler was last seen sitting forlornly in La Napoule harbour with a notice nailed to her mast, which meant she was not allowed to be taken anywhere. Anyone who bought her would be liable for the back payment of tax, not to mention the overdue maintenance costs, which effectively sealed her fate.

1982, and back at the factory all was not well. I couldn't blame the girls – they were only being loyal to their manager – but I do wish that one of them had dropped a hint about Graham. It wouldn't have taken much to bring Eddie and me to our senses. But then perhaps we should have seen the signs for ourselves. There were enough of them.

The fact that, despite being "on a strict diet", Graham's top drawer and briefcase were always stuffed with packets of digestive biscuits should have told us something. And the fact that the factory was always in darkness whenever we passed despite his protestations of working till midnight should have set alarm bells ringing. Whenever we brought up the mystery of the dark factory, he would ask what time we had passed, and, quick as a flash, would say that that was the moment of the power cut, and he had been under the stairs with a torch, attempting to fix it! How gullible we were.

The crunch came when he and I were manning a stand at one of the innumerable trade fairs we attended at Birmingham's NEC. I can't remember how, or why, we got involved in trade fairs. It must have been when we needed to start selling again, instead of sitting on our backsides letting the orders wash over us.

Fairs are a whole book in themselves. You quickly learn which ones you should attend, and the Harrogate Toy Fair in January was definitely to be avoided. Harrogate is beautiful, and we could travel daily, but the show was vast, and full of TOYS! Large acres of next Christmas's top sellers, and salesmen in metal suits from Solihull. In February and September it was the turn of the Gift Fair. This was usually held in either the NEC or Earls Court, and was much more our scene. But our favourite was Top Drawer, held in April and September, which was as the name implies.

I enjoyed designing the sets. One year we did Sloane Street, papering the entire stand with brick wallpaper. Another time we recreated an Icelandic scene with yards of white fur and Eddie dressed as a penguin in white tie and tales. One year, feeling very British, we had large Union Jacks everywhere. Forests, zoos, highland glens – not a problem, I made them!

However, the logistics, not to mention the cost, are horrific. For many thousands of pounds you are allotted a postage stamp sized space, wedged between a stand selling naughty chocolates, and one selling musical boxes. You have to park a mile from the hall, and are given a three minute slot in which to drive to a given door, unload and wheel all your paraphernalia to your stand, only to find the carpet layers rolling vast tubes of carpet down your aisle. By which time the tannoy is blaring out your registration number, with threats that if your vehicle is not moved immediately you will be barred for evermore. The facia board is spelt incorrectly, the electrics don't work, there's a large stain on your carpet, and an even larger notice telling you that on no account must you use, nails screws, glue, Blu-Tack, staples, Sellotape or drawing pins on the walls. Somewhere on the stand you also have to have a couple of chairs, a table, and – hidden from view – a niche for your handbag, coat, sandwiches, thermos, brochures, price lists and customers' files.

Having done all this preparation, you then spend four days suffering back breaking, leg aching boredom. You wait for hours, hoping the Harrods buyer will glance your way, and can guarantee that the minute she appears you've either got your mouth full of egg sandwich, or have just been cornered by a lady who's always wanted to meet Paddington's Mum. Some buyers flouted the law and brought their children, and whilst they were busy ordering their Capodimonte lamps, sent them to play on that nice stand full of bears!

The evenings we spent in a little hotel in Atherstone were amongst the happiest I ever remember. We met the same crowd each show, and would sit late into the night round a large table, either drowning our sorrows, or celebrating a good day.

Anyhow, I digress. At any trade fair there are long, boring periods in the day when no one passes your stand, let alone stops to make an enquiry. To pass the time, you prattle aimlessly with your colleagues, whilst at the same time trying to look bright and perky just in case a customer appears. This particular show at the NEC was no exception, and Graham and I found ourselves in just such a lull. Conversation was ebbing between us, he had given me chapter-and-verse on the itchiness between his toes and which remedy was best for his flatulence, so I steered the conversation towards business. I casually enquired how the orders for the Beanies were coming along. He said we had 1,000 orders on the books, and that he had placed an order with Gloria at Bury Masco for the fur with which to make them. "Seven bears to the meter isn't it?" I enquired, knowing bloody well it was. "Correct," said Graham, "so I've ordered 7,000 meters of fur."

Now, maths has never been my strong point, but I was fairly sure that to get the right quantity of fur, he should have divided 1,000 by 7, not multiplied by 7. Graham argued the point for some time, but slowly the face around his beard turned beige. "Just off to the toilet," he said and headed swiftly in the direction of the telephones. I knew damned well he had made an urgent call to Gloria, and it was confirmed later that our order with Bury Masco had been cancelled.

The incident worried me. If Graham could get such a simple thing so badly wrong, what else might he have done? On returning from the NEC, I made an unscheduled visit to the warehouse. The piles upon piles of fur in there were breathtaking. I placed an urgent call to Gloria.

She said that as well as the stock sitting in our warehouse we had £75,000 *worth of fur on order with Bury that had yet to be delivered.*

The news hit me like a bucket of cold water. Sometimes in business, you know instinctively that things aren't right, but you try to convince yourself that it's all in the mind. It wasn't. Graham was summoned urgently to Home Farm and asked to bring all his costing files and computerised analysis with him, in a wheelbarrow if necessary. He arrived the next day and we began to look through the paperwork. One of his costings read something like this:

One P.B. unstuffed £1
One P.B. stuffed 95p
One P.B. stuffed but naked £1.50
One P.B. stuffed and dressed £1.35

When we asked how a stuffed bear could cost less than an unstuffed one, and how a dressed bear could cost less than an undressed one, he admitted it was an error on his part, a bit like his error in calculating our fur requirement. As was the fact that he left the factory every afternoon at 4.59pm, and, according to the staff, if you didn't let him down the stairs first, you were in danger of being flattened.

There were minor discrepancies in the petty cash too, but these were relatively unimportant compared to the major blunders, I'm afraid I lost it.

"Keys on desk!" I said.

"Fat arse downstairs!"

Those were amongst the more polite phrases I used, but I remember resisting the urge to kill, purely because I enjoyed being a magistrate too much.

I never saw Graham again, but about ten years later I had a call from a friend who was Secretary of the local branch of the Conservative Party enquiring if I knew of a certain Mr Graham Pugh. Apparently he had been appointed treasurer of the club, and had milked the fruit machine of £5,000 for four consecutive years. In his last year, he was too greedy and took £10,000, which was spotted. He was caught, and the money was finally recouped from the sale of his late mother's house.

Eddie and I had to take quite a bit of the blame for this sorry state of affairs (not the fruit machine episode, I hasten to add). We had appointed Graham without taking up references; we never made the sort of checks that any sane bosses would have done; and we left him in charge because we wanted to be free of the everyday pressures involved in running a factory. His gift of the gab and his phenomenal self-belief just convinced us all was well. Rogue he may have been, but you couldn't blame poor old Graham. Having recently learned of Graham's death, all things considered, I know he was a rogue, but a very clever rogue, and you couldn't really blame him. We were stupid to employ him in the first place.

Chapter Eleven – Disney and Other Disasters

I suppose, looking back, we were beginning to panic. By the early eighties, sales of Paddington had dropped alarmingly to about 600 a month in 1982, compared to 6,000 a month in 1978.

When people ask me the reason for the drop in sales, my immediate reply is that no sales graph continues upwards forever. Eventually, it has to peak and then fall. By the eighties it certainly seemed to us that everyone in the world had got a Paddington and that we were on the other side of the peak. Sometimes I read that Paddington was knocked off his perch by the Teletubbies, but this is SO far from the truth. It's true that low cost bears were flooding in from the Far East, but Paddington was in a different league to them. I like to think that he simply took early retirement.

At the time of writing, Paddington is poised for a comeback. Michael Bond has written a new Paddington book, and Warner Brothers has bought the rights to make a Paddington feature film.

For a manufacturer, slowing sales are a nightmare. You have to keep your expensive machinery and staff busy, but churning out unwanted products is a fool's game. Equally, reducing your staff and producing fewer goods may save costs, but downward spirals are hazardous and you run the risk of being short of stock.

This was the situation we faced in the eighties. After Graham's departure I was now back in the driving seat of Gabrielle. Eddie was not well, and his passion for the business had waned. I would come home after a hard day at the office, pour out my woes, and he would offer his opinion on what I should do. The trouble was that we didn't always agree. On the question of Paddington's price, for instance, I thought that if we raised the price too high sales would fall, thereby defeating the object of increased profits. I wanted to keep prices within reach of the ordinary person. Eddie, on the other hand, argued that we should respond to the new market conditions (i.e. falling sales) by increasing the price and quality of our bears, thus making them rarer and more sought-after. Set back a bit from the day-to-day business, he could see the big picture. He could see that we were simply not holding our own, and that it was only the royalty income we were getting from Eden Toys in America that was keeping us afloat. I was slower to grasp this truth – reluctant to, I suppose.

It was frustrating for Eddie to sit by and watch me floundering about, designing quite unsaleable (albeit very attractive) items – fluffy penguins, pink pigs, pandas, polar bears, giraffes, gollies. I even tried to re-introduce the original turtles and tea cosies in a new range of colours. Hideous colours. I didn't realise how fashion had changed over the years, and what was a bestseller in the sixties was a dead duck by the eighties.

I think it was about this time that I decided to take on Walt Disney. Now, the Disney Corporation is a very different cup of tea to Michael

Bond. No cosy chats over the Chablis, or lunches at Le Caprice. I designed the full range of Winnie the Pooh characters: Pooh himself, in a hand knitted cardy! (got to keep the outworkers busy), Eeyore, Tigger, Piglet, Kanga, and Roo, and marched into the Disney headquarters in central London. I cheated a bit by plonking a Paddington on the desk first, which immediately impressed whoever it was interviewing me. I don't think there were any A.A. Milne characters licensed in the UK at that time, and the idea that I could make the same success with them as I had done with Paddington must have excited Disney.

I don't remember the financial intricacies of the deal that we eventually did, but I do remember that Disney insisted on a down payment of thousands before we were granted a licence, and then a royalty figure had to be paid on each sale. By now Joanna was a qualified solicitor and I took her along to one of the many meetings with a view to haggling. What a silly idea that was: Disney is not a human. It is a bell metal organization incapable of negotiation.

Once we had signed the contract, we had to produce prototypes for Disney to approve before we could go into production. Whereas in the past, design conferences had involved Michael and I sitting with a glass of wine in the garden, chatting convivially about PB, the equivalent meeting with Disney's design team was like going ten rounds with Mike Tyson. They employed ferocious women who seemed to take the greatest delight in tearing my ideas apart limb from limb. I would emerge from meetings with them convinced I was the worst designer the world had ever seen. Quite frankly, I doubt any of them had ever seen a Pooh.

And getting approval was just the beginning. We then had to do the really hard work of sourcing the fabrics, installing new machinery, and explaining to staff exactly how the new characters had to be made. It was exhausting and expensive. For instance, we had to buy new knitting machines specifically to knit Piglet's green and black striped vests and Pooh's cardigan. The black stripes on Tigger had to be screen-printed on, and then each part of his body cut by hand. We ventured into the world of velvet, never before visited, and encountered all the knotty little problems of fraying. Where possible, we used material we already had to make the Pooh products – the Draffakilla's feet became Eeyore's mane, for instance – but this wasn't always possible and most of it had to be newly sourced and acquired.

The sales as far as I can remember, were reasonable – we tried to rise above the run-of-the-mill market by designing a limited edition of 2,000 'Classic Pooh and Piglet' sets in a beautiful box – but production costs were not. Boxes full of red cardigans coming back from the outworkers had to be pressed, sewn up, and buttoned. Cutting the Tigger parts was hugely labour-intensive. Kanga's gussets kept fraying, and every five minutes someone from Disney would ring to say they were not happy with the positioning of Piglet's eyes.

It wasn't long before Disney performed the usual big company trick of wriggling around its contract. It unilaterally granted a licence to another toy company to produce a Pooh range, but whereas my designs were called 'Classic' Winnie the Pooh, the new range was called 'Plush' or 'Original'. Our lawyers assured us that this was a breach of contract. We could have sued Disney, but we'd have lost, and probably have run out of money before the case came to court. It would have been a David and Goliath battle, but without the happy biblical outcome. The cheaper range duly appeared on the market, made in Taiwan or somewhere in the East, and retailed at a price which completely undermined our products. And that was that.

The Classic Winnie the Pooh and Piglet.

On reflection, I think my heart just wasn't in Winnie. Perhaps it had something to do with the fact that I never met A.A. Milne. I have always adored his stories, but putting the characters into three dimensional form didn't give me a buzz. I was trying to fill a vacuum caused by the decline in sales of Paddington.

The introduction of Golly also caused us enormous grief. People were always telling me how, as children, they had loved their 'golliwog', as they were called then. Ignoring the storm of protest that had blown up over Robertson's Jam mascot we launched a superb Golly. Nothing but the best as usual – he had the most expensive fur hair, probably mink, and a coat of the very best red felt, a large spotted bow tie, and a *broidery Anglaise* frilly shirt. He really was magnificent, and was proving to be a winner, when the inevitable happened. A muesli-shoed do-gooder from Islington saw one in a shop window, and alerted the media. As we sat watching TV one evening, the six o'clock news started with a close-up of Golly. When Big Ben stopped bonging, the reader, in censorious tones, announced the grim news: a racially offensive toy was being sold in a gift shop in London! Mr Beardie was then interviewed, clutching Golly by the throat, and proceeded to threaten fire and frogs on the manufacturer who had come up with such a vile and offensive product. I have taken quite a lot of criticism in my time about my designs, but had never before had them described as vile. I'm not sure now whether or not bricks were thrown at the shop, but I do remember the retailer ringing us the next day to place a big order for more, as he had been inundated with requests. People from all over the country were delighted to have, at last, found their beloved Golly. We were, of course, ordered to stop making them. I don't know who gave the order, presumably the Golly enforcement department, but we completely ignored it.

🐾 🐾 🐾

I have no recollection of when or how we became involved with the Orient Express train, but we were asked by someone, somehow, somewhere, to design a bear representing the steward on their trains. VSOE, which stands for Venice Simplon-Orient-Express, commissioned us, and we made numerous trips to that building on the South Bank with the big golden balls on the top. 'The Steward' was a very smart gentleman, in a royal blue suit with brass buttons, a pillbox hat with scrambled egg round it, a white shirt, and black bow tie. The company agreed to source the brass buttons for us, as they had to be embossed with the VSOE logo, and we did the rest.

For his black shoes, we used the boots left over from junior PB. We had his enamel badge made locally. The bear himself was in the finest mohair fur – there was no shortage of that around Yorkshire. And we ran some braid down the sides of his smart trousers. There was some expense in getting cutters made for all the various shapes, but overall it was a straightforward project, production-wise. Certainly a lot easier than Pooh and friends.

Commercially it looked sound, too. The bear was to be sold exclusively on the trains, alongside other Orient Express gifts: monogrammed glass wear, leather handbags, silver fountain pens, onyx paperweights and so on. It was all terribly upmarket – there would be no tacky plastic 'Orient Express' ashtrays here. We were confident that if we produced an attractive bear, the rich punters on the train – a captive market – were bound to buy one as a memento of their trip or to give to their families. And we *did* produce an attractive bear. Yes, we were proud of our 'Steward'.

VSOE were a nightmare, though. There was a dragoness of a lady at their headquarters who was, I suppose, their quality control officer. Not a day went by that she didn't ring with some complaint or other. The hats were not glued on straight, the buttons were not sewn on symmetrically, the seams had not been brushed out sufficiently – there was always something wrong.

The relationship really soured when, for some reason, we ran out of 5mm black satin ribbon for the Steward's ties. Luckily we had stock of 7mm black satin ribbon. "That'll do", said Max, our enthusiastic manager at that time, and I had to agree. We couldn't hold up the despatch date, because a thousand Stewards were booked on a ferry to France, where they were to be stored in a warehouse in Dunkirk. So 7mm ribbon it had to be.

As required by our contract, we sent the dragoness a sample from the batch for scrutiny. She must have had her slide rule to hand, because the different size of the ribbon was instantly spotted. She phoned to complain vehemently that the ties were too wide, and what were we going to do about it? We apologized and explained that we had only used the 7mm ribbon because we'd run out of the 5mm size, "no harm done, ha ha ..." But no amount of trying to laugh it off worked.

"The bears will have to be recalled, at your expense, and dressed in the proper ribbons," she insisted.

"The bears have already crossed the Channel!" I said. "They're on their way to Dunkirk. It will cost thousands!"

"That's not my problem," she hissed.

We had no choice. I was damned, though, if we were going to transport a thousands bears back to Doncaster, and hit on a good idea! June, my trusty design assistant, a remarkable lady, whose beautiful and charming daughter was tragically killed at the age of eighteen in a car accident, was always game for an adventure, so I suggested we travel to Dunkirk, remove the bears' shirts (they were only false fronts, stapled at the back of the neck) and replace them with a thousand correct new "dickies" complete with 5mm ties which we would take with us. Simple!

We crossed from Harwich to Calais, and drove to Dunkirk. Arriving at dusk, we managed to find the warehouse in the docklands area of town. It was too late to start work that night, so we stopped at a hotel on the main road and asked if they had any rooms available. The woman at reception said they were full, but if we went round the back and rang the bell on the green door, it would open and she was sure we would get rooms. We did. It was the local brothel.

June took the room on the first floor, and I headed for the third. The lavatories were quite a way down the passage, but if you were quick and remembered your shoes, you could get back reasonably dry before the light bulb automatically switched off. I don't remember ever having seen such dirty sheets, or scum so thick in the plughole, but we were exhausted, and were pretty sure we wouldn't be disturbed by any clients (we weren't), so we bolted our doors, and tried to sleep.

The next morning we headed for the warehouse with our load of replacement dickies. We had been fantasising all the way about "Monsieur" who would no doubt take us to a little bistro for a light lunch, so it was disappointing to be greeted by a grumpy warehouseman who let us in then locked the door behind us. There was no heating in the place, and at twenty bears to a box you can imagine how high the pile was. We beavered away all morning, and by early afternoon had completed the task. All the shirts had been replaced, and the bears repacked and sealed in their cartons. Monsieur let us out and we made a dash for the lavatory.

Arriving back at Calais docks, we were herded into lanes, and a sticker with '4' on it was slapped on our windscreen. The douanier approached these two suspicious looking women, stuck his head through the window, and demanded to know where we had come from. Being tired and confused I said "Dieppe" and June said "Dunkirk" simultaneously.

"And when did you arrive?" he demanded to know.

"Last night," we said.

Looking at it from his point of view I suppose it must have seemed strange, two middle-aged ladies travelling to France for one night, especially as they didn't seem to know where they'd been.

He then asked us where the other two passengers were. "We haven't got any passengers," we said. Apparently the 4 sticker on our windscreen denoted the number of people in the car. Well, we didn't know that, and there was sod all we could do about it. Things were already going badly, but when he asked us the reason for our visit, I knew they were going to get worse. It's not often you get the chance to tease a French customs officer and I was determined to enjoy it.

"We have been to Dunkirk to change a thousand teddies' dickies," I said.

At that point, it became clear that Monsieur Douanier didn't have a sense of humour. He ordered us out of the car, and demanded to look in the boot. Now, I didn't think this was a good time for June to offer him a peppermint, but I could see her intentions were well meant. When we produced a plastic bag from the boot with a thousand mini shirt fronts in it, there was really nothing he could say, except that in thirty-five years as a customs officer he had never heard such rubbish.

I think Steward retailed at well over a hundred pounds, and our theory that the wealthy clients of the Orient Express would buy him as a souvenir regardless of cost was, I'm afraid, wrong. Sales were poor. Passengers must have felt that, having paid through the nose for their trip, they were not going to splash out another hundred quid on a keepsake for themselves or their darling grandchildren. VSOE's orders with us dwindled, and, once again, we were left with a nasty stock overhang – in this case, reels of gold braid and 5mm black satin ribbon!

Nor was this the last entry in the list of 'Gabrielle Designs That Didn't Work'. One of the latecomers was a design based on a series of books by Michael Bond about an armadillo called J.D. Polson. He was the first armadillo to be President of the United States, but was so lonely that he decided to give it all up, with help from A.A. (Armadillos Anonymous), and the C.I.A. (Central Intelligence Armadillos) and go back to live in Dilloville, Texas.

Once again, a delightful character, but not one that immediately brings to mind a cuddly toy. I hate the expression 'cuddly toy' from the days when it was used *ad nauseam* on *The Generation Game*, but I did my best to design an armadillo, having first thumbed through a few of the children's nature books to find out what one looked like. His shell was made from strips of felt in various shades of brown, his body was fur (no problem) and he carried a blue Pan-Am bag with the airline's logo printed on it. I imagine we probably contravened a copyright or two there. Inside the bag was a chocolate-coated bumblebee; that was the labour-intensive bit. We made them from yellow pom-poms with hand-painted black stripes, little glued on goo-goo eyes, and wings made of God knows what.

The problem with the armadillo was that Michael's books were aimed at the adult market, and children couldn't appreciate their humour, so our toys fell between two stools. Retailing at around £16, they were a complete flop. And what do you do with a thousand or so obsolete miniature Pan-Am bags, and a dozen sacks full of bumblebees?

Some time before, we had bought a large, disgustingly filthy, derelict building near the factory, in which to store the thousands of yards of fabric, hundreds of rolls of pink fur, and countless bags of stuffing that we used. The Pan-Am bags and bumblebees were dumped in there.

It wasn't unusual to be burgled around Doncaster, and burgled we were. Thirteen times, in fact, in our time at The Bear Garden, so it was nothing to get excited about, but when they hit our storage depot it was different. The intruders quickly realised that they weren't going to gain much by stealing bags of industrial waste and hideous flannelette, so they decided to have a bit of fun instead. They unrolled all the pink fur on the floor, emptied their bowels, then jumped up and down on it. We had to leave this charming scene in place, untouched, until the insurance assessor came. She must have been a busy lady, because it took her a few days to arrive, by which time you could smell the evidence in Doncaster. After examining the fur, the insurance lady asked why we needed to destroy it – surely it was washable!

Of the other twelve burglaries, the most memorable was one that took place one Christmas. When we received the call from the police they told us they had done a thorough search of the premises and had found nothing untoward. I rang the security firm and asked them to go and reset the alarm. Half an hour later the security officer rang, and said he thought I should go over and take a look. The family were staying with us at the time, so I set off with the children. When we got there, we saw that the entire back wall of the office and a large window on the first floor had been demolished, the radiator ripped off, and the partition walls (built of breeze blocks) between my office, the general office, the canteen, and the staircase had all got large holes in them. Water was cascading from the broken pipes, all the machines, including a large photocopier had been dragged down the stairs, and removed through a smashed back door. They must have known that if they opened any door the alarm would go off, so they decided to take the direct route through the walls. Every room was knee-deep in rubble, and when the little constable came in to take a statement, having first asked my age (vitally important in burglaries), his first question was,

"Can you actually spot anything you suspect to have been moved?" Good job Jeremy was with us. "Only the entire bloody factory," he said.

I have great respect for the police, despite their warts, but they struggled to maintain my respect that night. They had obviously driven to the site but because it was a bit cold and windy they didn't get out to look round the back of the premises, and assumed all was well. I seem to remember we did get quite a long apology from their boss.

Apart from Paddington, there was one design of which I was really proud, and which enjoyed moderate success, though it brought with it the usual amount of grief. We launched it in the early eighties, around the time of Hooray Henrys and Sloane Rangers, the Fulham-based yuppies made popular by the best-selling *Sloane Ranger Handbook*

This sort of strong social stereotype was a gift to us. We designed a 'Henry' with a Viyella check shirt, an old school tie, a flat tweed cap, a Barbour, and green wellies. He pleased me enormously. And, for once, we had a non-Paddington product that sold well: the SW6 crowd had plenty of money in the eighties, and Henry was the perfect gift for either sex. And didn't they look good on the mantelpieces of Battersea flat conversions!

There was, of course, a fly in the ointment, in the shape of a well-known designer who owned a shop in the Hooray heartland of Walton Street, near Harrods. If I remember rightly, she actually bought a quantity of our Henries to sell in her shop, but then, out of the blue, contacted us to say that she had invented the concept of the Sloane Ranger bear, that she had had the idea of making them for sale, and that we had infringed her copyright.

This was pure nonsense. Any fool knows that there is no copyright in an idea. It's the person who gets off their backside and does something about it that gets the rights. So bugger off madam. Solicitors were involved as usual, and a few tempers were lost. I can't remember the outcome exactly, but I never go down Walton Street today without a little finger gesture.

One project which brought us enormous pleasure (and of course the inevitable threats of legal action!) was the creation of an elephant for the Manchester Fire Service. The city's Metropolitan Council had given their fire service what I think is known as a corporate identity. The symbol they chose was 'Welephant' – a bright red elephant, wearing a yellow fireman's helmet, black boots and a belt supporting his axe. This mascot was then adopted nationally, two life-size Welephant costumes were made for promotional purposes, and some poor sod who drew the short straw would parade up and down the high streets of major cities with a bucket, collecting funds for underpaid, and undervalued firemen. Gabrielle Designs was invited to create a gift Welephant wearing the same outfit.

Welephant, no wonder we didn't sell many!

Once again we didn't think things through! It was a fair bet that members of the Manchester Fire Service would buy one, as possibly would a few firemen from other divisions if their children screamed loud enough, but let's face it, it was never going to be a world beater. Ever the optimists, we took the project on.

Jeremy was our salesman in the South by this time, covering the country from The Wash down. He mainly visited shops before 4pm, and planned his route carefully to finish within easy reach of that evening's party in Fulham. Boutiques in Penzance had to open their doors to him before 9am or never get a visit. He went down a bomb with most customers, but the odd few, those without a sense of humour, did ring us with complaints. His petrol expenses were ludicrously high, and he wore out tyres at a horrific rate, but he was happy. I think.

One of the things that made him unhappy was working weekends, but one Saturday Eddie put his foot down and insisted that he was to meet a very important buyer from overseas. The rendezvous was in a hotel foyer in Oxford Street, and Jeremy's brief was to show her samples of Paddington, Poulson, the pigs, pandas, etc. and get an order if he could.

They met at the appointed hour and everything went smoothly until Welephant was produced from the bag. The buyer was exceptionally unimpressed, and asked who in God's name he was. Jeremy feigned incredulity, how could anyone not have heard of the famous red elephant! "They are everywhere!" he said.

Our son is renowned for his good fortune, but this stroke of luck takes the biscuit: at that very moment in Oxford Street, the poor man in the Welephant suit that morning was desperate for the loo, so nipped into the hotel in search of the bathroom.

"You see," said Jeremy, as Welephant walked through the foyer, "here comes one now."

Still on the subject of dead ducks – not Jeremy – our next venture was Bothy. It was the year when the indomitable Sir Ranulph Fiennes had just completed his trek across the Antarctic. He had arrived home seriously short of funds, and his dear wife at that time, Lady Virginia, asked if we could help. She had a little Jack Russell called Bothy, who had accompanied her to the base station from where she gave Sir Ranulph support. They were childless, and this dog obviously meant a great deal to both of them. Once again Jeremy was dispatched to open discussions before I met with the pair to finalise a design. It was a bit reminiscent of Keith Michell. Sir Ranulph and Lady Virginia knew exactly how they wanted the finished product to look, but had not taken into account practical details such as where to buy Jack Russell fur. Bothy was to wear a smart navy blue jacket, upon which was sewn a Union Jack, and the Transglobe logo. He had a sweet little pink suede tongue, which was a good way to use up Batty Bat's wings!

We took the commission on, against our better judgement. Bothy was incredibly difficult to make, to stuff, and to sell. I think we sold about eleven, one of them to Prince Charles, who didn't strictly BUY one. He was attending the premiere of the film made of the expedition, and we were granted permission to set up a stall in the lobby of the cinema. Jeremy manned the stall with his girlfriend at the time, who turned up in a see-through dress. I think this is probably what brought the Prince over to the stall, but he was, as usual, terribly polite, and went off with a Bothy under his arm. The agreement was, that the expedition fund would receive 10% of our profits.

Which came to precisely nil.

The nearest to a nervous breakdown that I ever came was when we foolishly undertook to supply Marks & Spencer with a bear that was to be incorporated in the hoods of children's anoraks. The upper halves of the bears had to be in pink and black. Their heads sat on the front of the hood, and the arms hung down the sides, fastening under the chin.

Before you begin production for M&S, they send someone to inspect you. Fingernails, lavatories, health and safety posters, the lot. Then after a dozen or so samples have been submitted, and numerous adjustments made, you start. Late delivery of goods results in not just in a severe reprimand but threat of immediate cancellation of contract. Excuses, as I found out, are simply not tolerated. When two hundred arms came back from our outworkers with a twist in them, and a key worker took the day off to have her spaniel's ears cleaned out, I sat in the factory all night with a quick-unpick, frantically trying to rectify things. Their quality control may be second to none, but the M&S buyer in this instance got it sadly wrong: Mums don't buy black for their toddlers, well they didn't even like the pink either, so thank goodness they withdrew the orders. Nowadays, whenever I buy an M&S garment and have cause to complain, I spare a thought for the poor sod responsible for making it.

Chapter Twelve – My Sad Years

The start of the nineties brought a mixture of joy, worry, sadness, and frustration. Jeremy and Joanna were happily married, and Eddie and I had moved out of Home Farm to a large farmhouse in the village of Eddie's birth, called Tickhill. Shortly afterwards, both children spoke the words every parent longs to hear, "Get out the knitting needles Mum!"

Eddie's immense joy was quickly overshadowed by his increased pain. He had been diagnosed with osteoporosis, and his asthma was so bad that he had to use a nebuliser every day. He could no longer even think about the business, and whenever I talked about it he became frustrated at what he saw as my blind optimism. It concerned him that we had never set aside money for a pension. It didn't concern me – I always maintained that I would work till death and Gabrielle Designs should us part, and presumed that the accountant had put a lump sum somewhere which I could dip into when required.

Back in the early seventies, I was recommended to put my name forward for the Magistracy, and although I agreed I had no confidence in being accepted, so I put the idea to the back of my mind.

In Doncaster they are very careful to appoint magistrates that form a balanced Bench in terms of class-creed, colour and political persuasion. Postcodes seemed to be important too.

Around that time, they obviously were top-heavy in some respects, and I wasn't needed as ballast until 1980, when out of the blue I received my invitation from the Lord Chancellor!

My work as a magistrate provided me with a welcome escape outlet from pressures at home and work. This was an important part of my life, and I'd advise anyone who has their own business to cultivate an interest outside their work. If you don't, your business will simply devour you. When you enter the holy sanctum of a magistrates court, all thoughts of factory, husband, and children, are forgotten. You are addressed respectfully as "Ma'am" and inhabit a world of smart suits, court shoes, and make-up, which made a welcome change from my usual factory wear. The staff apparently always knew if I was sitting that day, because I had lipstick on!

The job itself was intellectually demanding, often interesting and occasionally boring. You have to concentrate hard on the task in hand, which can be difficult when the advocate for the defence is droning on and on, realising he's on a sticky wicket and repeating everything three times – presumably once for each magistrate. It's getting close to 5 o'clock and you really want to get to M&S before they close.

Most, but not all, of my fellow magistrates impressed me. Quite a few joined the bench for entirely the wrong reasons, and it showed in the way they carried out their responsibilities. There were men, for instance, who had clearly been henpecked all their lives, and saw the bench as a way to assert their opinions and restore the authority they had lost at home. This type were terrible listeners, often bigoted, and wore incredibly ugly shoes. Then there were the women – the ones who had *done* the husband-pecking at home – who used the court room as a place to continue dominating and domineering others. Unattractive.

The third type were those who were determined to get on the honours list at all costs. Unfortunately, they often succeeded.

A fourth type is politically motivated. I well remember one new magistrate with very greasy hair, who announced on her first day that she would never send anyone to jail. I am not of the "hanging's-too-good-for-em" school of thought, but I did think that her dogmatic stance against prison sentencing, before she had heard a single case, was a bit presumptuous.

I am certainly not saying that I was perfect. I am sure my fellow magistrates found me wanting in many respects.

The training for the magistracy is intensive, time-consuming, and can be very boring. For the first two years you are 'on the wing' (i.e. learning the ropes as one of the two magistrates sitting either side of the chairman). All you have to do is stay awake, look reasonably intelligent, and nod approvingly whenever the chairman whispers something to you. You keep notes of the proceedings, or in the case of one of my colleagues draw the most fantastic cartoons of the defendant. I never made notes because one of my very few skills is remembering the spoken word – an attribute which annoyed Eddie immensely. I could always repeat every word of an argument, and he had no chance.

When you have served two years on the wing, and provided you haven't committed any crime that would upset the Lord Chancellor (especially drink driving, although he didn't like speeding much either), you were invited to train as a chairman. This could sometimes involve re-enacting court proceedings, with the clerks taking the roles of advocates and defendants, and you in the chair. And you were videoed. At the end of the training, the tapes were played back, and the chief clerk invited your colleagues to criticise your performance. It could be deeply humiliating. Grown men were known to weep at these sessions, and they certainly didn't do much for one's morale.

I remember my first sitting as a wing magistrate so well. I had to lead in, and walk (with dignity) behind the chairman's chair to get to mine. I was wearing my smartest suit, which unfortunately had a belt secured with belt loops at the side. I managed to get one loop caught on a stud behind the middle chair, and had to spend what felt like a week unhitching it, with all the ushers, solicitors and clerks remaining bowed.

My very first case involved a man who was accused of standing naked in his front window as children were walking to school. He pleaded not guilty to indecent exposure, his lawyer arguing that he had not in fact been naked, but had been wearing underpants. The lawyer then produced as evidence a pair of Y-fronts, in Royal blue satin, with a large orange carrot printed on the front. We had been told at our training sessions never to let our facial expressions reveal our thoughts: no sighing, no raising of the eyebrows, and above all no laughter. I am afraid to say that on this occasion, we failed the test.

The first moment I realised that I needed glasses was in court. I was in the chair, and on reading the court lists for us that day, was horrified to see that the first case was one of buggery. Never having dealt with this before, I thought we ought to seek advice from the court clerk so I requested a short adjournment, only to learn that it actually read "burglary". I was down to Specsavers that afternoon.

I don't want to give the impression that court life was one long sequence of pratfalls. Most of it was serious stuff. But it's the embarrassments that stick in the memory. One afternoon sitting, I hurried back from a quick lunch in the salad bar. My habit at the time was to wear my glasses on a chain around my neck. As I took my seat,

I raised the spectacles to my nose end, to find a complete slice of hard-boiled egg stuck to one of the lenses.

At the age of sixty-seven, with another three years to go before compulsory retirement, I realised the time had come to quit. The amount of mail I was receiving from the Home Office each morning was prodigious – the law seemed to change every day. Magistrates were not expected to be solicitors, but we still had to read all the new orders and legislation, and it took up too much time. Sentencing was also becoming much more complicated. When I started, the options were simple: a fine, borstal, or for more serious offences, prison. By the time I retired, there were countless programmes that had to be considered: anger management courses, unpaid work requirements (Community Service in my book), activity requirements, alcohol retreatment, attendance centre orders of varying lengths, curfews (a waste of time), drug rehabilitation, exclusion orders, and so on. And instead of simply asking a non-payer-of-a-fine defendant if he had brought his toothbrush, you had to consider an operation pay back programme.

I left the fines enforcement court after realising I was becoming too cynical. The lies we had to listen to about their hardships, knowing they smoked sixty a day, and had been "done" for drunk and disorderly countless times, were a joke. The usual magistrate's trick was to sentence them to three months prison for non-payment, but to suspend the sentence for ten minutes. If, in that ten minutes, they paid the fine, they didn't have to go to prison. It was amazing how many of them had an Aunty Doris, or some stupid pregnant girlfriend in the gallery who came up with the money at the last stroke.

On my last day as a magistrate, I sobbed all through my retirement speech, all through afternoon court, and all the way home. I was going to miss it, but was slightly aggrieved when the prosecuting solicitor said in open court, before the proceedings started, that I would be sadly missed, because I was always such a laugh. I am sure he meant it kindly, but I didn't like to think that my legacy after twenty-two years was to be remembered as no more than a joker.

I can't imagine how I lived in the weeks leading up Eddie's death. Joanna was pregnant, big time, and Jeremy's wife Francie, small time. Business was not good, and Eddie seemed to be trying out every hospital in the North of England and a few in the South. We never really had any diagnosis, let alone cure, he was in great pain, sleeping most of the time, and the medics in the village didn't seem to care very much.

Joanna and her husband Jon had moved into a new flat in Battersea, or Fulham, or Clapham – I can never tell where one ends and the other begins. The properties along the Northcote Road seemed to vary in price according to how many minutes walk you were from Clapham Junction, and as Jo and Jon were both commuting to the City every day, they had to choose between a long walk or a big mortgage. I went down to help decorate the nursery, which, after all is one of the joys of becoming a grannie, but it meant leaving Eddie alone, and he was getting weaker by the day. The factory must have been running on teacakes, but I had the two stalwarts, Pat and Joan, in the office, and a great crowd of girls.

Eventually, Eddie went into a nursing home in Sheffield for assessment by a specialist. After a couple of weeks, they finally diagnosed bone cancer. I am sure he had had it for ages, but that the doctors who saw him were happy to content themselves with osteoporosis, and never felt the need to investigate further. He returned home, but was confined to bed. That was 1994, and I bought my first mobile phone so that I could keep in contact with him during the day.

A course of chemotherapy was prescribed for Eddie, but we all knew in our hearts that it was far too late. He was transported by ambulance to Sheffield and I followed by car. Jon rang me on my mobile as I went up the M1 to tell me Joanna was four centimetres dilated! In my excitement I lost sight of the ambulance carrying Eddie, and followed another one, to the wrong hospital. Joanna will tell you how long her labour lasted – many days – but I don't remember anything of that week. I think Jon does.

Eddie was getting very confused, the chemo was making him sick, and when I went in with the news that our first grandchild had been born, his main concern was whether or not I knew at which market stall to buy the food for our pigeons. How cruel life is, that the thing you have longed for comes at the very moment when your brain is unable to comprehend it. Benjamin Edward was born on May 7th 1994, and Eddie died on May 21st. Poor Jo, she always maintained that she hit the height of joy and the depth of misery within one week.

I rang Jeremy the night before Eddie died to prepare him, and in true Jeremy fashion, he left the dinner table, and jumped in the car. In true Francie fashion, she wrapped the hot chicken they were about to eat in foil and threw it in the car, so that we had something to keep us going that night. It was still hot 160 miles north!

We didn't tell Jo how close her father was to the end until the next day. Francie picked the three of them – Jon, Jo and Benjamin – up from Clapham, and Jaguared them up the M1 at great speed. Even in that day of misery and grief, we saw humour. They arrived at the hospital and emerged from the lift, Joanna with her baby stuck on one breast,

Jon, who has never been famous for his elegant appearance, in an interesting shirt, Francie, seven months pregnant, with a short denim jacket over long shirt and boots, and carrying two enormous Asda bags crammed with coke and doughnuts. None of us had washed or seen a comb, or slept for that matter. We were ushered into a side room before we frightened the other visitors, and specialists kept opening the door, apologising for having got the wrong room, and hastily retreating. They obviously thought we were a crowd of gypsies.

Eddie was able to hold Ben for a few minutes before he died.

Two days after Eddie's death, Jeremy went to Sheffield to collect the death certificate. It was a foul day, cold and drizzling, and he remarked to the registrar that he didn't want to visit Sheffield again in a hurry. The registrar was visibly affronted, "But we've got the Supertram!" he protested. Somehow, Jeremy didn't think that South Yorkshire's electrified bus, however state-of-the-art, adequately compensated for his father's passing.

Exactly two months later, on July 21st, Jeremy and Francie's first child, Emily Harriet was born.

Chapter Thirteen – Jekyll and Hyde

As I knew they would, my family and friends kept me sane in the months after Eddie died. It was like living in a vacuum, but you keep going, because quite honestly you don't have a choice.

It wasn't until I was throwing out all the dead flowers which had festooned the house, that I found a card, attached to an enormous bouquet, which read: "With deepest sympathy, Stephen and Lorraine." Not having a clue who they were, I rang the local florist, and was told that the bouquet had been sent by the Beaumonts. Still none the wiser, I asked around if anyone knew who the Beaumonts were, and was told they were the couple who ran a design and printing firm called Letterflex on the industrial estate near The Bear Garden.

I was touched. I had done some business with them – they printed the labels that went on our bears including the *Please look after this Bear* labels – but hardly knew them at all. I mean, you wouldn't forget Steve in a hurry. He had the longest waxed moustache I'd ever seen, sported flamboyant bow ties, and sat behind a large glass-topped desk, upon which stood nothing but a leather writing case, and a silver pen. I do remember my first meeting with him, because he told me he could never start work in the morning until his pen was positioned at right angles to the edge of the desk. Now that basically tells you all you need to know about Steve. Or so I thought.

A few days later I dropped round to his office to thank him and Lorraine, and at the same time I ordered more printed labels. As you would imagine, his workmanship was exquisite, his manners impeccable, and the glorious Lorraine always supplied me with a beautiful china cup of coffee. His premises were a bit of a let down – just a prefabricated shed on an unadopted road full of potholes and puddles, situated between a motor repair shop, and a pile of tyres.

As we chatted, Steve remarked how he envied my lovely factory site, and would dearly love to buy it. In jest, I replied that he was welcome to the site, provided that he also bought the company. The conversation went no further, but my offhand remark had been received and filed, as later events showed. Eddie always said that I would never find anyone daft enough to buy Gabrielle Designs, but then he didn't know Steve.

Subconsciously, what I'd said to Steve must have reflected my real wishes, because after Eddie died, my commitment to Gabrielle Designs plummeted. I struggled on, and the staff were fantastic, but my passion had gone. Why was I driving fifteen miles every morning to stand behind a factory bench tying bows round Jane Churchill bears' necks?*

Over the following months I became heartily sick and tired of stuffing. I resented being woken up in the middle of the night to be told that The Bear Garden burglar alarm had gone off again. I was the sole key-holder, and the police would only remain on site for twenty minutes

---

*We made hundreds of bears for Jane Churchill in her fabrics and with satin bows round their necks. I still maintain that I am the only person who knows how to tie a bow tie properly.

after calling me. No matter how quickly I pulled on my knickers, and how fast I drove up the M1, I could only do it in twenty-one minutes, which meant I had to open up the factory and search for the robbers alone.

I was sick of it all. Building up a business from scratch is great, developing it is all-consuming, and then suddenly you wake up one morning, and there it is, like a great big millstone hanging round your neck. A millstone can be removed and thrown in the sea, but with a business it's not as easy as that. The property assets can be disposed of quite easily, but you've also got thirty or forty people whose livelihoods depend on you. You can't just walk away; it's there behind you like a shadow. You never imagine when you start out that this problem will ever arise – you're so busy you don't have time to think about it. But look out if you're a young entrepreneur. It will. Take note of the emergency exits early on.

Perhaps Steve sensed my disenchantment. In any event, after that first brief discussion he dropped in to see me at The Bear Garden at every opportunity, and was always charming and sympathetic. He would bring up the subject of buying Gabrielle Designs in a light way at first, but pretty soon the discussion became serious.

At some point, he and Lorraine invited me to have dinner at their heavily stencilled cottage. I have never been one to tiptoe around subjects or to negotiate 'tactically', so anything they wanted to know about the business I told them, from the practical aspects of bear stuffing right down to the financial nitty-gritty. As far as I was concerned, their interest in Gabrielle Designs was very welcome – like a lifeline being thrown to me, in fact. They must have liked what they heard, because at the end of the evening they announced that they would definitely like to buy the business.

I was advised by everyone, and we both agreed, that I should employ Steve for about nine months as an assistant, so that we could get to know each other, and he could learn the 'art' of Paddington, as it were. If at the end of that period we were still both keen, we would move towards a sale of the company. It didn't take him five minutes to move in, leaving his printing firm in the capable hands of Lorraine. He came in like a lion, stripping my office of clutter (I didn't have a silver pen positioned at right angles to my desk). He set up his own little work corner, and devoured all the stock books, accounts, and sales ledgers. He was meticulous in every way. And most importantly he had a great sense of humour, which has always been my number one criteria in choosing anybody for anything.

Another attribute which impressed me was his devotion to his two daughters from his first marriage. They lived in Dorset and he and Lorraine went down every other weekend to stay with them, without fail. The girls at the factory all loved him, although he didn't spend much time on the factory floor – he was happier in his office, straightening his desk.

I had a little difficulty restraining him, he was so full of enthusiasm. He had visions of designing Paddington in sombreros, Bermuda shorts, kaftans, and Santa Claus outfits, and thought I was very unimaginative in sticking to the duffle coat, rugger shirt rule.

I felt that before we went any further down the road I should take Steve to meet the powers that be. Firstly, of course, he had to meet Michael Bond, because there was no question of his running Gabrielle Designs without approval from that quarter. We were invited to lunch at Michael's in Maida Vale. Steve wore his best shiny khaki suit, with the most vivid of his bow ties, and commented on the nice "dinner wine". Michael is one of the most polite and dignified gentleman I know, and when he phoned me the next day he simply said, "What an interesting man, Shirley. Where *did* you meet him?"

We then ventured to Oxfordshire to meet "the revered Nicholas", Michael's agent with whom I had had many a spat in the early days. Steve had the gift of the gab and spouted financial jargon all afternoon – I think he must have been on a course to learn 'business speak'. He talked to Nicholas about his plans for Gabrielle and, as far as I could tell, Nicholas was convinced.

After nine months, things were progressing well. I felt able to leave Steve to deal with orders, and customer complaints, and it was brilliant to have his help at trade fairs. He was anxious to get his hands on the reins, so he approached Lloyds Bank in Lincoln to see if he could borrow the capital to buy the business.

It was about this time that Jeremy and Francie took a long break, somewhere far away, and asked me to take care of Emily. She was only nine months old, so I took her with me each morning to the factory, and she either sat in her little car seat in our office, or the girls took it in turns to push her about in her pram amongst the fluff.

One morning, with ice on the ground, I deposited her in the office, and rushed back to the car to collect my bag. My feet went from under me and I fell, hitting my head with a resounding thud on the tarmac. People rushed out and heaved me up, but what I didn't realise was that the Bank Manager had arrived from Lincoln and was interviewing Steve, who by this time had a screaming Emily dribbling over his shoulder. I was too concussed to talk much sense, but managed to be polite with torn tights and blood pouring down my leg.

Obviously, the bank required a business plan. I can never see the point in them, because you can say anything you want about your plans, and the projections can be completely pie-in-the-sky. Steve's read like Aesop's Fables part two! There was almost nothing he wasn't going to achieve in the next twelve months. He would bring out hundreds of new designs, would be selling around the world, would double the turnover in the first year, and planned to buy out Marks & Spencer, from what I could gather. The bank people were hugely impressed, and although it seemed to take ages to finalise the loan, they agreed to provide the money he needed. One of the provisos, I think, was that I should remain as a consultant for five years on a very generous salary for two days a week. Steve also had to use a Business Manager as a sort of guarantor and he was to be paid vast amounts to attend one day a month. I often wondered why!

Joanna was by now a fully-fledged corporate lawyer and a partner of a firm in London, so she undertook to conduct the sale. A meeting to discuss terms was convened in her offices, with her brilliant senior partner in the chair. A wonderful character, he had a broad Scottish accent, one eye, and a rude tie.

Steve arrived first. It was a warm day so he had removed his khaki jacket, and simply wore a waistcoat he had designed specially for the occasion. It was silk, and on one front had a hand-painted picture of Paddington with acrylic red Wellingtons, and on the other, a jar of marmalade. Across the shoulders and down the back were paw marks.

Lorraine arrived late. She had obviously been to the hairdresser to have her roots done. She wore her shortest Chanel suit in pale pink, her lowest cut blouse, and a silver ankle chain. The eminent senior partner, in his sober pin-stripes, muttered in an aside, "Joanna, where the hell did your mother find these two?"

Steve kept slapping me on the back, and saying, "We don't need legal agreements do we Shirl? We trust each other", which is just what solicitors want to hear. Anyway, we managed somehow to agree terms, and all the necessary "legals" were put in place.

I can't remember why the completion meeting was held in Nottingham, but sometime in March 1995 we all gathered in some lawyer's office in the city. Joanna came up by train, and I arrived by car with a bunch of yellow roses to give to Lorraine as soon as we had signed. I remember sitting for hours, a bit like you do when completing on a house deal, waiting for the bank to ring and confirm that the money was in my account. It all happened, I kissed Lorraine, Steve said congratulations, and that was the last civil word that he ever spoke to me!

Joanna and I left the office, and skipped down the main street of Nottingham hand-in-hand, singing. She was just as excited as I was. She and Jeremy were co-directors of Gabrielle Designs so they stood to gain a little financially, but I think they were just very relieved that I had managed to remove the millstone from around my neck.

Elated, I decided to leave my car where it was and we both caught the train to London, drank Champagne all the way down, then met up with Jeremy, Francie and Jon, and drank ourselves senseless. It was gone, it was no more, and the coffers were full. No more worries!

How wrong we were.

Chapter Fourteen – The Collapse of Gabrielle

Having sobered up, I returned home, and prepared myself for the role of consultant. I thought it would look rather good on my passport, 'Design Consultant'. I left Steve alone for a week, thinking it would be tactful to let him settle in. When I finally visited The Bear Garden, I was told that Steve and Lorraine had left for a two-week skiing holiday the day after they bought the company. I thought that a bit strange.

Soon after they returned, a row of brand new purple cars appeared in the car park – one for each director, I presumed. I am not quite sure who was on the board. Joanne, a silent girl with long dark hair down to her thighs, seemed to have some position of responsibility, and Lorraine's mother was lurking around the place. The builders moved in very quickly, and demolished the beautiful canteen, which had been the pride and joy of the girls. They were told to bring packed lunches and eat them at their machines, amongst the fluff presumably. The canteen was transformed into Steve's office and a magnificent conference room, with a fitted carpet and a large boardroom table, around which were placed twelve superb chairs. There was a smart coffee machine, a water cooler, and at the head of the table the statutory writing pad and silver pencil. My workroom, in which I had done all my designing, cutting out, and sewing had gone, and had been absorbed into the conference room.

Downstairs, the main factory room had been divided across the middle, thus cutting out most of the daylight, and a new designer – don't know where she came from – had been installed in the front section. The stuffing machine had been moved into a cupboard at the back.

Walking around like survivors of a battle were thirty shell-shocked workers. Twenty-nine actually, because Pat, the accounts clerk, had taken one look at Steve and walked out.

Steve had imported most of the staff from his design company to The Bear Garden. They were unfriendly, silent young men, seated in front of newly-installed computers on very expensive chairs in the room which we had previously used for finishing off bears: putting Pooh in his cardigan, fitting Henry with his green wellies, dressing the Orient Express bears with their dickie bows, or – a job which I never trusted anyone else to do – putting the sealing wax on the knot of the string tied around the box of the 'Classic Limited Edition Paddingtons'.

These tasks now had to be carried out, along with everything else, in the darkened half of the old main room. Joanne seemed to be the boss in that department. I think she became Steve's third wife.

Hundreds of new bears were in production. On my first visit I remember bears in Burberry and Aquascutum mackintoshes, with their distinctive plaid fabric and beige gabardine. There was no disputing that Steve could generate business, but he lacked any ability to see orders through to production.

I hadn't been there two minutes when he ordered me to design an owl, *by Friday*. What had been my office was now a sewing room, my scissors had disappeared, and when I asked Steve where I was expected to work, he pointed to the old store room. No table, no drawing board, no pencils.

If I wished to speak to Steve, I had to make an appointment through his secretary, and if I was lucky, would be allowed to see him in his office, which should not to be confused with the conference room, though it was equally sumptuous.

I could see things were going to be very tricky, to put it mildly. The girls were beginning to mutter discontentedly; some of them had even lost their chairs to the conference room. I spent as much time as I could in the workrooms, where I had always been happiest. I tried to ensure that at least the Paddingtons were being produced to the usual high quality. Almost any other designs I produced were rejected by Steve out of hand. He was only interested in the new designer downstairs. She was rather glamorous!

At the end of my first month, I can't remember what my monthly salary was, but it was presented to me, with deductions! Twenty minutes pay was taken off for late arrival, the visit to the dentist also cost me dear, and there was a deduction for "time wasting, and disruption of the workforce"! It was difficult to argue because Steve had left for an all-expenses tour of Australia. We knew what a wonderful time he was having because his picture appeared in all the trade magazines: Steve wearing a baseball cap with Paddington on the front, Steve touring Sydney and Melbourne. The only trip Eddie ever made abroad at the company's expense, apart from the ill-fated trade fair in Cologne, was the day he went to France and overindulged on oysters with our agent. The only trip I ever made was the one to

Dunkirk to replace the ties of 1,000 Orient Express Stewards. Steve, on the company's – that is, the bank's – money, was living high on the hog from Day 1.

Crisis point was soon reached. One morning in his office, he lost his temper completely, flew at me, and rushed down the stairs into the warehouse where Lorraine found him sobbing with rage on a bale of stuffing. This was madness. I decided to cut my losses and run. Quality of life was far too important. I agreed to accept £5,000 and disappear, which I did.

I would never have believed that a man could change his whole personality in a day, and in one of our many "discussions" before I left, I asked him why he had suddenly changed. My own view is that he was a Jekyll and Hyde character who was capable of putting on an act to suit any situation. He certainly had me fooled, although in retrospect I think some of the staff had got the measure of him.

The storm clouds gathered ominously over Gabrielle Designs. Almost as soon as I left, I started receiving frantic calls from my old suppliers asking if I could help to secure money owed to them. They had always been used to prompt payment, and were threatening to withhold further deliveries until their accounts had been paid. I learned that stocks of stuffing, wellingtons, and fur, were all running dangerously low at The Bear Garden, and much more seriously, the staff were not receiving their wages. Steve had managed to persuade them to hang on, each week giving them a plausible reason for the delay.

I had given Steve twelve months before I was sure he would go under, but he managed to keep the company going for two years before one morning the girls arrived at the factory to find half the equipment gone, together with Stephen...Surprisingly, no sign of Joanne either. Lorraine, his wife, showed great strength in adversity! She took over the reins and despite having no experience at all, managed to keep the business alive. It was a short-lived reprieve, and in February 1998 Gabrielle Designs went into receivership.

The news was reported in the press and on television. There were melancholy scenes of the girls leaving The Bear Garden for the last time, weeping. One was physically sick.

My one big regret is that I let down my wonderful, loyal staff. I had to sell the business, because I couldn't go on forever, but in my heart of hearts I knew Steve was not going to succeed. And when he went down, he dragged the livelihoods of so many wonderfully loyal people with him.

I heard later that Steve and Joanne had bought a house in the village next to me in Nottinghamshire and that he started yet another company in Sheffield. If it ever floats on the Stock Exchange, I shan't be a shareholder.

Bear business: Mrs Clarkson with the Paddington she made in 1971

Paddington, the bear now departing with 21 jobs

HE HAS been adored by adults and children alike since the day he arrived from darkest Peru.

But a host of television and Disney rivals have ousted Paddington Bear from the affections of today's younger generation.

His declining popularity has forced the closure of the only British factory making cuddly versions of the lovable bear. Gabrielle Designs, where Paddingtons have been made for more than 25 years, is due to go into liquidation next week with debts of more than £300,000 and the loss of 21 jobs.

The firm was started by Shirley Clarkson, 63, who made her first bear for her son Jeremy — now a household name himself as the presenter of BBC TV's Top Gear. Recognising the potential of the marmalade-sandwich-eating character invented by author Michael Bond, she acquired the world rights to make and sell the bears, initially at her Yorkshire farmhouse home and later in a factory at Adwick, near Doncaster. Mrs Clarkson, who sold the firm in March 1995 to Stephen Beaumont and his wife Lorraine, described the closure as 'very sad'. She added: 'Paddington was British from top to toe. He will probably be made in the Far East in future.'

While Mrs Clarkson still has the original Paddington she made in 1971, her son has moved on to racier hobbies.

'As far as I'm aware, Jeremy no longer has a Paddington Bear,' she said.

The end of Gabrielle Designs. © Daily Mail, 1998.

Chapter Fifteen – Reflections

Looking back on the last 50 years, I have so many memories, some happy, some not so happy. The details fade as the years go by, but the personalities of the people stay as vivid as ever:

First and foremost, Eddie who began the journey with me and travelled so far; Michael Bond, who gave us our big break; June and Kristina, my stalwart sewers; Joan and Irene in the office; Gloria at Bury Masco; Mr Ormerod at The Lancashire Sock Company; Martin the beanie manufacturer; Eunice our incorrigible cleaning lady … the list is a long and colourful one.

On that list, underlined, are my children Jeremy and Joanna, who never asked to be part of the story, but who played a key role. They inspired me to start designing, they endured Gabrielle's rollercoaster ups and downs, and they were there to prop up Eddie and me in the difficult times.

I am without doubt very lucky to have had such an interesting and fun career. At the still-ripe old age of 73 I've realised that if you don't enjoy life it's not worth living. Actually I realised that a long time ago, which is perhaps one reason why I have enjoyed myself.

Since retiring, I have emigrated from Yorkshire to Northamptonshire to be near Joanna and her family, and I can make it to Jeremy's in an hour and a half. One of my greatest joys is watching my grandchildren in their various school activities. I am healthy, play a lot of tennis, have a great social life, enjoy renovating property, and love to return occasionally to Yorkshire where, let's face it, my roots remain.

When it is my turn to go to the great Stuffer's Paradise on High, and I am accounting to St. Peter for my actions on Earth, I will tell him of a conversation I had on the train one day. The lady sitting opposite asked me what I did for a living. I said that I made Paddington Bears. Instead of the usual reply – "You must have made a fortune!" – she said, "You must have brought so much pleasure to so many people."

I hope she is right, and that it will be enough to get me through the Pearly Gates.